The Forgotten Soldier

Soldier

By Bruce McEwen

Chapter 1

If children came with a maker's stamp when they were born, then I believe I would have come into this world stamped "Made by the British Army".

I was born in Iserlohn British Military Hospital, Germany, into what you would call a typically dysfunctional British Forces family. I was the youngest, with three older sisters. Dad was a mechanic in the army, a Scotsman who worked hard and played hard; mum originally is from Yorkshire. I was fortunate to grow up in a loving and close family who, like any forces family, had their ups and downs and their calamities. I spent the first five years of my life in Germany, where my dad was based. We moved around a few homes and I have vague but happy memories. One of my earliest memories was of Christmas 1982, when my dad got me my very first Scotland football strip with my name across my back. How I loved that strip and how proud

I remember feeling when my dad saw me wearing it. I was quite a character growing up and had no trouble finding mischief - or in other words mischief had no trouble finding me.

I was never one for coming down our stairs in the conventional way, but had mastered sliding down the banister that was attached to the wall. On one particular morning, nearing the bottom of the stairs, my foot unfortunately got stuck between the banister and the wall. Here is me stuck and in an awkward position. My dad's friend and neighbour had to come in and rip the banister off the wall to get me free. This was but the first of many calamities I would find myself in. As I said, I don't have a lot of memories from Germany, but I do remember for a period of time there was just me and the youngest of my sisters with mum and dad, as the two older sisters were at boarding school in England. Fond memories I do have of Germany were the summer barbeques and socials between the families and how they would go on late into the evenings. Being forces families abroad, there was a real community and family spirit.

My dad got a posting to England, so the family caught the ferry and moved to Bulford near Tidworth where he was to be in charge of the army mechanical workshops. Dad was doing well with his army career and had progressed up the ranks to Warrant Officer Class 2, even showing potential and recommendation to become a commissioned officer. I made friends quickly and settled into my new school and army home. The resilience of military families, especially children, was that we were flexible and adapted to the regular moves of home and schools that came with our fathers being in the military.

An old milk float used to do the rounds on the estate where we lived. The milkman looked like an old character from Emmerdale with the biggest sideburns you could imagine. Back then it wasn't uncommon for us 'army brats' to be allowed onto the float. The estate was hilly. One day the milkman was doing his rounds and we were all playing on the float. It was parked on a hill and, unbeknownst to me, one of the kids went into the driver's cab and accidentally released the handbrake. We all felt it moving and jumped off. All we could do was watch in shock and horror as this unmanned milk float headed downhill picking up speed, then suddenly it caught someone's drive and smashed into a local resident's car. We ran - I mean we ran for our lives - my mate Garry and me bolted for his house where my mum was having a coffee with his mum. Apparently, the look on our faces was pure shock and we wouldn't say a word when questioned "What's wrong - what's happened?". I mean, how was I going to keep this from mum? The walk back to my house was horrible. Mum took one look at the carnage and knew exactly what calamity I was involved with. Apparently, all my mates accused me, as the policeman was at our house asking me for my side of the story. As years went by mum revealed to me the policeman was struggling not to laugh when he was going door to door interviewing the kids involved. This one of many calamities that would seek me out.

As a family we had barely been in England for two years when dad came home with the exciting news; he was posted to Hong Kong and we would be going too. I had never been anywhere like that before, let alone even on a plane. I can tell you, the whole family were excited, especially mum. Our last few weeks in England were so exciting for me, we went and spent some time with my Uncle Brian and his family in Kent before we flew out to Hong Kong. They took us to London and we saw all the sites which, never having been to London and at such a young age, I thought it was amazing, especially seeing the Palace and the soldiers stood to attention outside. All too soon we had to say 'goodbye' and head to Heathrow to fly to Hong Kong on our new venture as a family. I was excited but yet anxious at the same time, as I had never flown before - and what an experience it was to fly for the first time at only seven years old.

To this day I will never forget the experience of the humidity hitting me when we stepped off the plane at 3 am in Hong Kong. We were to live in a high-rise block of flats and I remember a couple of dad's army colleagues were there to pick us all up and take us to our new home. Even their wives were already there getting the flat ready for us when we arrived. As I said before there is real community between military families and they all get stuck in and help each other. Like family, we are all in the same boat, forces families having to follow our dad's/husbands around the world with the army. It wasn't long before we settled in and really loved being in Hong Kong. The new exotic smells (and so not exotic smells); Hong Kong was like no other place. It was literally a 24-hour city with new, modern westernised world alongside traditional Chinese custom and culture. It was certainly something else, and we were blessed to be there for 2 years.

We lived on the mainland in a place called Kowloon, but as a family we would frequently get the ferry across to Hong Kong Island and explore and experience what it had to offer. One of the fondest memories I have of Hong Kong is many a time sitting with dad on the balcony at 3 in the morning, watching the world go by in the cool morning breeze. We lived on the top floor and we had an amazing view. I really cherish the memories of that time with my dad, sometimes we would chat and put the world to rights, sometimes we would just sit and be quiet, but all the same I loved my dad and I loved my one-to-one time with him. I loved all my family and had amazing unique relationships with all my sisters and my mum.

But there is something special about time together as father and son. In Hong Kong I was to enjoy many special opportunities to have that one-to-one with dad. For me, dad was my hero - he still is to this day. I looked up to him, yearning for his love and his approval. My dad was not one to speak of his emotions; he certainly didn't say he loved me. But deep down I knew he did and he wasn't one to hold back affection from me.

I have many great memories; walking up Lion Rock with dad, or going for walks in the park, or going with him to watch him play football. But sadly I also had many memories of him being away a lot, or not coming home until very late and not seeing much of him at times - getting confused as to why mum was angry at him not being home. Sadly, dad liked a drink, and he spent a lot of time in the Sergeants' Mess drinking with the lads instead of being home. I want to share one particular memory that was very key in my life as I look back now. I was eight years old and was sat with dad chatting about death. I remember asking dad what happens when you die and I remember dad saying to me that when you die you are just no more. This scared me right to the core and I became frightened of death. I would get so upset and frightened that I would cry in the shower, calling out 'if there was a God don't let me die, I will be good I promise, let me live forever'. I truly believe God was listening back then and put in motion His plan and purpose for me. It was, for me at that time, a really scary period of my young life.

One of the things about living in Hong Kong as a military family was that it was very social. We were always out as a family at weekends, at Sunday lunches in the Sergeants' Mess, going out on outings around Hong Kong or socialising with other families. It was a very busy and active time. Even with my primary school, I got to see a lot of Hong Kong and see and experience Chinese culture and customs. As I said previously, mischief had no trouble in finding me and I got up to all manner of mischief. I was regularly brought home by the Military Police for being up to no good. I was forever in and out of the military infirmary with stitches to my head or for x-rays for the mishaps I got into. One particular incident I recall was hilarious, but not for my oldest sister. She was the head girl at school, going out with the head boy and 'in' with the popular crowd. There was a park where we lived, surrounded by the high-rise flats; this was the hang-out for all the kids. In the centre was a small building that housed the Chinese takeaway, with a pub and restaurant around the back. It had a tin roof where they would dry the fish. I remember playing on that roof and my sister telling me to get down calmly, trying to look cool and in authority in front of her friends. I remember shouting no and proceeded with a friend to throw the fish at her. I certainly got what for that night. Looking back, I was young, and innocent, enjoying my childhood and being a typical boy. It was a great time living in Hong Kong, but after two years it was time to head back to the UK.

Dad's last posting in his career was to Edinburgh. I was quite excited at the thought of moving to the Capital of Scotland. We flew into Edinburgh airport and got a bus from the city all the way down to Dumfries where Nana and Papa lived; my dad's parents. It was great to see them after two years away and we were to spend the summer with them while dad and mum headed up to Edinburgh to get our new home ready and to get a new car for us all. The summer went very quick and soon dad was taking us all up to Redford in Edinburgh, which was to be our last army house. I went to Colinton Primary School, and fitted in very quickly as the majority of the kids at the school were military kids too and all in the same boat. Football was the main thing for all the lads and everyone on a Wednesday afternoon would try and prove themselves and get a place on the school team. I tried my hardest and eventually got a place on the team for a few games around Edinburgh. But I truly wasn't a natural footballer and was trying hard to prove I was good enough. The fact was, my dad was a gifted footballer, having played in the army all his days in the military. I felt I was trying to get my dad's approval; that underneath I was as good as he was and that he was pleased with my performance. Deep down I knew I wasn't really any good and eventually gave up trying out for the school team. It was around this time that I started to realise I too wanted to be in the army when I was big enough, I wanted to be a soldier and the roots of this dream dug down deep in my soul.

One day in early 1986, dad came home with a brochure he wanted to show me. It was a glossy brochure for an all-boys military boarding school in Dunblane. Dad asked me if I would be interested in going and, looking through the brochure, I got excited at the thought of going to this school, especially if it meant pleasing my dad. Deep down I liked the look of the school and the thought of wearing a kilt and getting to learn to play the bagpipes. There were a few kids in my class at Colinton Primary whose dads had the same idea and were also considering going. I had to attend an assessment day at the school where we would be tested on our maths and English and also an interview with the school board, which included the school headmaster and commandant. I was very nervous but also felt safe as dad was with me during the interview. Afterwards we were shown around the school and all its facilities; I was so excited at the thought of potentially coming here. Then the dreaded wait came.

I had to wait about three months for the post to arrive, telling me whether or not I had been successful in being accepted. The day of anticipation came and the post arrived. Dad opened the letter and read out the news I had been successful and I would start at the school in the August of 87. Three of my school mates had also been accepted and we were all about to embark on a new venture in our lives. The summer was a very quick but busy one. Dad and mum bought a new house and for the first time in my life we would have a home we could call our own without the thought that we would have to move again in a couple of years. We moved a few miles away to a cul-de-sac in a suburb of Edinburgh called Currie and my parents still live in the same house to this day. My oldest sister had now left home to train as a nurse, my middle sister had a year left at high school so she would continue at her old one while my youngest sister went to the high school in Currie. For me I was about to start at my new boarding school in Dunblane and I couldn't wait.

"For the sons of Scottish Soldiers, Sailors and Airmen," were the words that on a sign that greeted us as we drove through the stone pillar gates and up the hill into the school grounds.

There were many new faces like me that looked like frightened sheep as we entered the house we were to be part of. The school was split into a primary house consisting of P6 and P7, two second year houses for S1 to S3 and a senior house for S4 to S6. I could feel the eyes of the oldest boys in the school looking at us rookies, like vultures probably thinking 'fresh meat'. We were all assigned a P7 boy to look after us and who we would bunk with in our allocated dorm. All of us rookies met our new teachers, shown where we would bunk and then taken to stores to get our uniforms, it wasn't long before our parents said their goodbyes and we were left to settle in.

It was very quickly quite a culture shock that this school was quite a tough school and there was a pecking order amongst the boys, with the weaker ones very soon weeded out and picked upon. Now I was not the biggest of boys and very gentle in nature and quite sensitive. I soon had to learn to toughen up, as I was very quickly one of the ones targeted and picked on. The regime of the school was quite a shock and tough, with daily room inspections and learning how to lay out our uniforms for inspection plus daily chores we had to carry out. Rugby was the sporting religion played at the school. As a rookie we had to learn to march and eventually have a passing out parade, where we would officially become Victorians (members of the school.) We had to either learn piping, drumming or Highland dancing. Realising that piping wasn't really for me I chose Highland dancing. I was to find I was actually quite good at it and had an amazing and very encouraging and supportive instructor, Miss Anderson, who made a huge impact on my life.

It wasn't long before I was getting beaten up on a regular basis by a couple of older boys who had taken a dislike to me. We learned quickly one thing you don't do is 'grass' on people as it was a big 'no-no' and brought serious repercussions. It was a real culture shock at age

10, being away from family for long periods of time at such a tough school. The first year went quickly and it wasn't long before I was heading into P7 and was responsible for looking after a rookie myself. It felt a bit easier, as the older boys who bullied me had now moved up into the senior houses and I was away from them, but I found that I would get picked on and beaten up by guys in my own year who liked to throw their weight around and I struggled to stand up to them. My confidence had taken a real dive now, but I soldiered on, as the saying goes, and put it down to being part of a tough school. During my first year I got involved with the scripture union run by Sister Wharton, the school hospital matron, a gentle and loving soul and just an amazing person. As it was an all-boys' school I ended up playing Mary in the school nativity and got stick for that for some time after!

During my time in P7 there was one teacher who was simply a legend, who didn't make an impact just on my life but many kids' lives at the school. His name was Mr Silcox and he was our school chaplain and religious education teacher. We had to go to church every morning, but each Sunday Mr Silcox would bring excitement and joy to the service with the amazing stories he would tell. He wasn't just our preacher but he was also head of the school shooting and owned machine guns. He was an amazing character but the most gentle and compassionate man anyone could ever meet. After P7 we all had the choice of moving up to either Trenchard or Cunningham house which meant a lot of us would be split up. I liked the look of Trenchard, so I chose that one which was on the top floor of the main school building.

Moving up to secondary was to become even more unbearable for me at the school. The bullying intensified and got worse. As a first year I was subjected to punishments from the house prefect. A lot of them abused their position and got away with it, as it only made it worse if you tried to speak up. I would have kit inspections thrown on me first thing in the mornings, where I would have to report to the prefect in whatever uniform they decided. I would be made to do push-ups or sit against a wall with arms out for as long as they deemed or got bored. If I started to slip, as it was very strenuous I would get a punched or kicked and made to do it again. They could be quite brutal and they got away with it. I would get a kicking for no reason at times just because they felt like it, and these 'punishments' would come at silly times through the night or at weekends.

t was also around this time that the constant bombardment of name calling and being called stupid and gay became relentless, with no reason behind it. I would find myself getting beaten up unprovoked in the night when I was sleeping by some of the boys.. I lived with the not knowing when or where or what time the next attack would come. At one point I courageously tried to get some of the bullies back one-to-one, but it was pointless as they would soon just gang back up on me and the beatings would be worse. The mental bullying was relentless and for me this was worse than the physical bullying as I could numb myself to the physical beatings. But the mental and emotional bullying goes right to the core and after long enough you start to believe the lies. For me I started to believe I was stupid and worthless and it really affected me.

The bullying got worse and worse as I went through 1st year to 3rd year. It didn't help either that it was the older boys who supervised us during prep (evening time in class doing homework) and even our sessions in Cadets. The kind of unprovoked punishments we would get from them would include having our knuckles rapped with the edge of a ruler. Or a a favourite for them was to draw a thick chalk line on the blackboard and we would have to put our tongue on the blackboard under it. They would then pull the blackboard down so we ended up having to lick the chalk as it came down. I would get punched in the head or kicked for no reason at any time. It was during these years of bullying that I slowly withdrew. I kept myself to myself. I started to misbehave in the hope I would be expelled, and I seemed to live in detention most weekends

At one point I did try to cry out to my parents that I wanted to leave and that I hated it at the school. My parents had a meeting with the headmaster and somehow, he managed to convince them that it would be best I stayed at the school and I wasn't allowed to leave. I never held that against them but as much as I love my parents, I truly felt let down and from then on, I knew I could not trust anyone. I completely withdrew into myself as time went on and the bullying continued. My behaviour got worse and I would then pick on other weaker kids out of my pain and anger for what was being done to me. I look back now and can see I felt suicidal, in that I wanted to die and I wanted the pain to stop. I already felt like I was a freak and so worthless and stupid from the constant mental abuse. I started to live in fear of when I would next be attacked at night and beaten up.

There were still days where, out of the blue, one of the boys who had it in for me would punch me right in the face when I wasn't expecting it. By the end of 2nd year my behaviour had become so completely erratic and out of control that the school thought I had behaviour issues and made me see a child psychologist, where I was diagnosed with dyslexia, but at that age being made to see a 'shrink' made me feel even more of a freak. I can tell you exactly why I behaved the way I did; it was in the hope that I could be expelled. I started to develop a coping mechanism for what I was going through. I started to self-harm, where I would hit myself in the head continuously to get release. I was so angry and I truly hated who I was and what I was letting these boys do to me, but yet I felt helpless to do anything about it. The pain I got from self-harm actually felt like a a short release at times.

Due to my low self-worth, one of the effects on me was to neglect myself and my hygiene by not showering properly or brushing my teeth. This neglect would eventually have serious consequences to my dental health for which I am paying for now as an adult. The strange thing is though, in all the bullying I was going through it never put me off or hindered my dreams to be soldier and be in the army. My other way of coping was shutting myself off from everyone and being alone as much as I could. But the bullying would not ease up. By the Christmas of 91 I had finally talked my parents around into letting me leave the school and I was so relieved that I did not have to go back in the new year, but I also believe that the damage had been done and the person I was when I left the school was far from the happy-go-lucky young lad that started at the school.

Chapter 2

It was a bit of an eye opener when I started at Currie High School, having been at an all boys' boarding school for the previous four and a half years. Having girls in my class was something I was not used to. From day one I kept myself to myself, only gradually making a couple of close friends. To be honest, I had no interest in school or even wanting to apply myself and do well. I had no self-confidence. I did not trust anyone and I had a real self-hatred, with a core belief that I was stupid and worthless. I felt that I did not have an identity that would say who I was. I was very withdrawn and struggled to interact or communicate with people, especially those I didn't know. I felt like a freak, even at my new school.

These were the consequences of the years of bullying I had been through. The one saving grace was that I got to go home at the end of each day and retreat into my sanctuary; my bedroom. I learnt to enjoy my own company, and I enjoyed going on my own for days out into Edinburgh, which for me I truly called home. I battled the hatred and anger that rose inside me regularly and self-harm became a way of coping. Sometimes, I would get myself into such a rage that I would hit myself repeatedly on the head, calling myself stupid. Afterwards, I would feel a release. On other occasions I would cut myself - on my upper arms so that the marks would be hidden - this also gave me a huge release albeit only a temporary one. These were cycles I went through for a very long time. I was now fifteen and searching for longing, acceptance and identity as to who I truly was. But I also felt that emotions were weak and brought me nothing but pain and misery. It was here that I started to learn to suppress everything and especially to suppress my emotions. I never had a brother to look up to and so I looked up to Ian, my brother-in-law; I admired and wanted to be like him. I still had a desire to join the army and join the infantry. My dream was to one day enlist into Ian's Regiment and follow in his footsteps. At sixteen I joined the Army Cadets for a period of time, enjoyed what it had to offer and, for a while, I felt I belonged to something.

At Christmas 1992, my oldest sister bought me my first set of dumbbells. I had my first taste of lifting weights and I instantly got the bug for it. I loved how my body responded quickly and I started to get muscles. I liked the fact that I was getting bigger and stronger and it was here that I first made the vow; I would never allow anyone to pick on me again. As I had no interest in school, when an opportunity came at aged sixteen that I could leave and go to college, I jumped at the chance. I now had a new-found freedom; I came out of my shell a little and enjoyed college life and what it had to offer, rather than mundane school and its strict rules. It was also here I discovered the college gym and became serious about my training, reinforcing my first taste for bodybuilding. My body really responded to the training on a whole new level and I started to get seriously strong and put on size. The vow I made to never allow anyone to pick on me again was cemented in my heart, and this was one of the roots that led me to start lifting weights. I was almost literally living in the college gym. I idolised the bodybuilders of the day as, growing up I had always idolised Arnold Schwarzenegger and I dreamed of having a physique like him. I started to bunk classes and was never really serious about studying, as I was finding my way in the world. I was also still battling with my emotions and bouts of dark depressive moods would come upon me, at times even making me feel suicidal. At times I felt that my emotions were out of control. I felt desperation, anger, worthlessness, self-hatred, that I was un-lovable, and a rage would try and rise within me. This made me even more determined to suppress my emotions deep down, especially as these bouts would lead me to self- harm to cope. I was doing a lot of things in secret, ashamed if anyone would find out. At a young age, at boarding school, I had developed an unhealthy pattern of masturbation, to relieve tension and to comfort me when I felt rejection and abandonment. This made me very embarrassed and ashamed.

Eventually I managed to get my first proper job, working in Burger King. I really enjoyed working there. The hit television series 'Gladiators' was in full swing on a Saturday night and how I longed not only to be as big as the Gladiators, but to have a physique as good as theirs! It was also a pipe dream to one day compete on the show. In the early part of 1994 I got serious about joining the army and joining the Infantry in my brother in law's Regiment. 'Soldier-Soldier' was also on tv at the time and I couldn't get enough of watching it. My room was plastered wall to wall with anything to do with the army; this was the only thing I truly wanted to do with my life. Deep down I also believe that I was trying to prove myself as a man and find identity as a man - a tough man. I felt that the army was where I would find this. I also wanted to serve in Northern Ireland; this was a dream I had always had. I don't know what it was, but something about serving on the streets of Belfast really drew me. As dad had served 3 tours in Belfast, part of me was probably trying to seek his approval and acceptance. So off I went to the Army Careers Office to apply.

The Recruiting Sergeant was welcoming and very helpful, especially as I showed interest in the infantry – his own background. I was told that I had to sit an aptitude test to see what job would suit me in the army, but I only had sights on the Infantry; nothing else appealed to me. I also believed at the time that the Infantry would make me into the tough man I longed to be. I filled out the paperwork and a few days later I went in to sit the aptitude test and, to my surprise, actually did very well. I had thought I was stupid and I didn't realise or see the potential that I really had. Going home and telling mum I was joining the army did not go the way I had hoped. Both of my parents were surprised at my wanting to join the army, especially as I had never seriously voiced this to them until now and after my sorry experiences at military boarding school. Dad was very supportive but I had a big fall out with mum when I told her I wanted to join the Infantry. She got quite angry about it and stated that in no way would she let me join the Infantry; that if I wanted to join it would have to be a in a trade. The problem was that at 17 years-old I needed my parents' consent to join, and no way was mum giving permission for me to join the Infantry. I didn't want to wait another year until I was 18 to join without their permission, so I thought I would become a mechanic like my dad. My thinking was if I followed in my dad's footsteps he would definitely be proud of me.

So the decision was made to join as a mechanic with my parents' backing and support. I proceeded with the selection process and passed all the fitness tests, medicals and interviews. It wasn't long before I took the oath of allegiance and I was enlisted into the army and on my way down to Woking near Reading to start my basic training. My parents took me there and stayed to see me off as I headed off with all the new lambs to the slaughter. I wasn't ready for how much of a shock to the system the army was to be or how much I wasn't ready for the army. In time, I realised that I wasn't mature enough for the army at this point in my life. Deep down, my heart wasn't in it to be a mechanic, I only chose this trade in my desperation to join up and not being able to be in the Infantry. The training was very tough, even though I was actually doing quite well, both physically and academically, learning everything that we were being taught, but deep down I hated it and was giving up and wanted to leave. I had chats with my training Corporal and Platoon Commander and even though they said I had a lot of potential and I would make a good soldier, that I should stick it out, I just wanted to leave.

After a month of training I got the opportunity to leave and headed back home feeling a total failure, believing I had let my dad down. I believed deep down that he was disappointed with me but I never heard him say it. Still, I felt a complete failure in leaving the army and not sticking it out. Giving up was soon to become all too familiar in my life and a constant theme that followed me thereafter. I went back to work full time at my old job at Burger King and after the summer I went back to college. I was just living life and trying to find my way in the world. Over the next year and a half, I would bide my time between college and working at Burger King, enjoying what life had to offer.

It was early in 1996 that I started to go out and start drinking. I would go to a club every Thursday with mates from work and it was here I started to get the taste for drinking and partying. I had no experience with women and I was still able to say I was still a virgin. I may have been very shy with girls, but I soon took to drinking to excess with no bother at all. I ended up getting myself into a rut in the way I was living - working in a dead-end job, going out and getting drunk regularly and having no real aspirations for the future. It was around early summer of '96 that out of the blue Steven, a friend from schooldays, knocked on my door and we went out for a drink. A real friendship sparked between us and we became best friends, forging a brother-like bond that is still as strong to this day. We became inseparable and would go out drinking together most weekends. His mum and dad treated me like a fourth son and would even go out drinking with his family regularly. Even though I was enjoying life now, I found myself in a complete rut and my life was going nowhere. I had come to a crossroads and truly reflected where I was going to go with my life. The dream of joining the army, of being in the Infantry, was still deeply rooted in me. I didn't need mum's permission now, so the plan was to go back to the Army Careers Office and join back up again, if they would have me that is. But that plan was to take a completely different path.

I was in town one afternoon, with another old friend from school, when he asked me if I would go to the RAF Careers Office with him, as he was planning to join them. While sat in the careers office I asked off the cuff what the RAF Regiment was all about; I'd heard a little about them at boarding school but didn't really know what it was they actually did. I was told all about them and how they were an infantry-trained Regiment that specialised in the defence of airfields and RAF assets, with the capability of taking enemy airfields. I was given a grest deal of information to take home and it got me thinking seriously. I then decided that it was the RAF Regiment that I wanted to join, as I had tried the army and I liked the sound of what this Regiment were all about. The conversation with mum when I told her I was going to join the Regiment was a repetition of our older discussion; she was not the least supportive about it. But this time it was my decision and it was what I wanted to do. Dad was supportive and encouraged me in saying that if this was what I wanted to do, then to go for it.

Eventually mum did come around and was supportive and encouraging when she saw I was serious and focussed in doing this. My thoughts were that the Regiment would finally make me the man I wanted to be, tough, strong, a man's man. I believed it would offer the lifestyle I always wanted and challenge me to be the best that I ever could be, I believed I had what it took to be a RAF Regiment Gunner; the tough man that I wanted to be. So, I got myself really focussed and as fit as I had ever been and threw my heart and soul into getting ready to join; I was out training at silly times in all weathers to get as physically fit as I could. I had to travel to RAF Honington in Suffolk which was the RAF Regiment Depot to undertake a selection course, to see if I had what it took and if I was what they were looking for in a potential Gunner. I passed all the fitness tests and performed well in the interviews; the selection team said I was exactly what they were looking for and were happy to offer me a place on the next recruit intake. Heading home I was over the moon. I saw myself doing nothing else and I knew this would be my life and become my identity. I had to wait until the November to get start training, as I missed the October intake due to administrative delays in obtaining clearance to join, having joined the army previously. November 12th 1996 was a proud day for me, as I was officially enlisted into the RAF Regiment and that very day travelled on the overnight train to start my new career and begin a new life.

I arrived at RAF Halton (the RAF's recruit training centre) with a large group of new recruits that were also on the train. Straight away we were met by RAF Regiment training staff who separated all the Regiment recruits from the other RAF recruits and formed us into an organised rabble to march off as best we could, given that many of these new recruits had never marched before. We were held at RAF Halton for three days in a blur of activity; getting issued our kit; learning to march in the drill hall; having our heads shaved and also having the pleasure of paying for it. We got to know our training NCO's and what sections we would be in, who our fellow section members were, and especially who was to be our section Corporal, who would be literally be taking us through our whole training. We all bonded very quickly and very soon some close friendships were established. We were all in this together, all from different backgrounds with different levels of experience to the military. One thing was for certain; we were all going to need each other and help each other in the coming weeks. Before we knew it the three days were up and we were transported to the Regiment Depot where the real work was to begin.

My first phase of training was a six week recruit phase, which was a blur of sleepless nights or very little sleep, averaging about five hours a night if we were lucky. The instructors' aim was to break us down so they could rebuild us to what they needed us to be. The days were filled from first thing in the morning, with room and kit inspections, drill, weapons training, physical-fitness training as well as basic soldiering and military knowledge. We were housed in twelve-man dorms so we all quickly bonded. The evenings were taken up with getting all our kit washed and ironed for the next day's inspection, making sure our lockers were tip-top. We were very lucky if we got a minute to sit down. By the time everything was turned around and the block cleaned to inspection standard, it was a collapse into bed at midnight, if fortunate, and then up at five-thirty to start all over again. We then had the pleasure of making bed-packs of our good old issued sheets and blankets, to be the right size and dimensions to meet the Corporal's standards.

No matter how well we prepared our kit for inspection, inevitably something was always found to be not to be up to standard and kit would go flying across the room; a mattress here, a boot there and so on. The Corporal would always find a reason to be in your face, to scream obscenities at you and tell you to get a grip and get it sorted. This was all part of the breaking-and-making process.

As new recruits we were not allowed off camp until we had completed that recruit phase. One term we became all too familiar with was that of being "beasted." This involved the whole flight (the RAF's name for a platoon) or section receiving a physical punishment of runs and press-ups and so on if anyone had got something wrong or wasn't paying attention. This became all too common throughout our training and we came to expect it at any time. The training was certainly tough and I really knuckled down, focussed and put everything into it; I made really close friends and I started to come out of my shell more. I started to experience belonging, acceptance and identity. I knew deep down that these guys I was training with would have my back, and I would have theirs. As the weeks progressed the training became more intense, but we were also learning more and more. We actually started to resemble a group of disciplined soldiers, but we still had a long way to go. My training Corporal, 'Simmo', was firm but he was also very fair as was my Flight Sergeant. Five weeks into training, after our first field exercise, we got two weeks off for Christmas, it was nice to head home and spend Christmas with family. Even though I was only five weeks into training, I somehow felt different and even my family noticed a change in me. I was finding my feet and purpose as a soon-to-be RAF Regiment Gunner; this was going to be my life and my very identity.

Christmas leave was all too soon over, and even though I had managed to catch up with my best friend Steven and have a good few sessions out drinking with him, I was eager to get back to the Depot and resume training. We enjoyed the fact that when we had all got back and resumed training, we only had a week of recruit phase, followed by a week of Adventure Training in Wales before commencing phase 2 of training. We had a parade at the end of recruit phase and then a long weekend. It felt so great marching off the parade square officially, no longer recruits, I felt a complete sense of satisfaction having completed this phase of training and remembering back to two years earlier having felt a complete failure and let down for leaving the army during recruit training. I had become good friends with one of the recruits called Mark, who was from Southend and had invited me to come to Southend with him for the weekend. His dad was brilliant and welcomed me like a son. I was made to feel like part of the family and this was to be the first of many weekends to Southend with Mark during training and even when we were posted to our first unit. Southend became a home from home for me and his family made me feel like family, in fact Mark was like a brother to me and I loved that they accepted me and loved me like a son, as I loved his family like they were my own.

I met Becky in Southend. She was to eventually be my 'first' and I thought that I loved her. However, it was never to work out how I thought it would, or how I wanted it to, and we were to end up just remaining friends. Adventure Training in Wales with the Physical Training instructors was a blast with many sessions drinking in the evenings. Then back to get serious about the next phase of training which was Trained Gunner phase, to take us from recruit to that of a trained military RAF Regiment Gunner. The training intensified and the physical training got much harder, but the training also became more exciting and so did the field exercises. Notably, we moved from twelve-man dorms to single-man rooms. The room and kit inspections were not as rigid or as frequent, but we were expected to keep everything up to the same standard (and better) at all times, as inspections could be thrown on us at a moment's notice. We were not recruits anymore and we were given more trust, but more was also expected of us.

Enjoyably, we were now allowed out at the weekends and to go to the local town; Bury St Edmunds. Also good was the fact that we were not the newest intake on camp any more, and a new batch of recruits had arrived. As the training advanced in all areas, including shooting which is the bread and butter of soldiering, the expectations got higher and there were targets we had to reach and pass. I was really throwing everything I had at it, reaching the standards required and excelling in some areas. My section Corporal was more approachable now and even though he was still very firm, he was very encouraging and guided me when I struggled in areas. I really looked up to Simmo and especially my Flight Sergeant. It wasn't long before we had reached the end of trained soldier phase and entered into our final phase of in 'Dismounted Close Combat' (infantry training).

Something that excited us about entering this phase was that we no longer used the iron sights on our weapons but now got to use the Sight Unit Small Arms, Trilux (SUSAT) sight that only combat arms got to use. This phase of training got really tough and the expectations and targets to meet became greater and harder. The field exercises were getting much tougher and we were now being trained in all aspects of modern warfare and the role of a RAF Regiment Gunner. I was really loving it and training hard and learning to play hard at the weekends. The fellow Basic Gunners on my course were like my brothers and we were a close-knit group when we went out drinking. At one point I did hit a low point and was struggling with who I was and if I had truly what it took to be a Gunner. I started to contemplate giving up, as I had always done in life, and considered leaving basic training. I owed it to Simmo and my Flight Sergeant who wouldn't let me give up, but encouraged me to keep going; that I had what it took to be a good Gunner and that I would do well in the Regiment. I listened very seriously and if it wasn't for them I don't think I would have completed the training and seen it through. To this day they have my utmost respect and taught me so much during my time of basic training.

We had bayonet training at one point; all the training staff 'beasted' the whole Flight and wound us up to get angry and aggressive enough to use the bayonet; during the training they pushed us to levels of aggression some of us never thought we had - that I never knew I had - this was channelled into bayoneting a simulated enemy in the form of a dummy. The whole emphasis of this training was to help us prepare for the day that we may have to face a situation of close combat in war and have to actually bayonet an enemy. After that training, my Flight Sergeant actually complimented me on how well I did and how he believed in me. That really went deep; I was moved by my Sergeant's belief in me and that really encouraged me. The training was soon coming to an end and I could see the finishing line. We had a final five-day exercise that put everything we had been trained in to the test, with literally no sleep and weighed down by about 80 pounds of kit we carried out our final Flight patrol of about six miles, then carried out a full Flight-level attack on a built-up mock village, after which we heard those much desired words "End-Ex." It was over, we had done it, we had made it. Well not quite officially just yet; we had to complete a week of field-firing at Sennybridge in Wales first, but technically we had made it.

The Flight travelled-to Wales to complete a week of live firing starting from pairs, up to four-man Fire Team, eight-man section attacks right up to a full Flight attack. This was the closest we could get to real soldiering using live ammunition without actually being in battle for real. This was the peak of all that we had learned and we were now putting it into practice. The week was amazing and I loved every minute. It went by so quickly and I could truly not see myself doing anything else other than being a Gunner for the rest of my life. Our last week of training was preparing for our passing out parade and we were all finally allowed to wear on our uniform our hard earn rank slides that had RAF REGIMENT sown on them. I felt such a proud level of achievement that I had made it, that I was soon officially to be a RAF Regiment Gunner. At this stage we were asked to list where we wanted to be posted, but the likelihood of us getting our actual choice was just a dream, hence we called it the 'dream sheet'. I put in for a posting to Northern Ireland but it came as no surprise when I was told my first posting was to be here at the Regiment Depot. But truly I was just happy to be in the Regiment.

April 23rd 1997 was one of the proudest days of my life, marching into the drill hangar with those who had completed basic training in our best blues with the elusive RAF Regiment 'mudguards' (shoulder-flashes) on our shoulders, I couldn't describe what I was feeling and how proud I was. All our families were there, including mine, to watch us all become official RAF Regiment Gunners. Standing to attention with my weapon at the shoulder I reflected on all my time through training and who I had now become. I felt I had become the tough soldier I wanted to be, that the training had taught me to suppress those emotions that were a weakness. I found purpose, I found identity. From this day on, the military was my life - I was now an infantry-trained Gunner. It was now, first and foremost, above everything in my life. This is what I saw myself doing for the rest of my days. Looking back from day 1 to this day I had changed; I had become what I was destined to be - tough, strong, a soldier ready to fight and die for my country, my Regiment, my mates; as the saying went "for Queen and Country." I was now ready to start my new career and after a quick two weeks leave at home, I headed back to Honington, this time not as a trainee but as a fully-fledged RAF Regiment Gunner.

Chapter 3

There were a few lads from my course who were posted to the same squadron. Everyone was arriving back in dribs and drabs and the banter and spirits were good as we were in and out of each other's rooms catching up. There must have been about ten of us posted to the same unit. We would all be split between the six flights on the squadron. James and I were appointed to F Flight; we were the two new Leading Aircraftsman (LAC) or 'sprogs' as we were known. The squadron I was posted to was assigned to protecting a highly secure compound on a four-on four-off rota, which meant that the perks were that we got a lot of time off. The novelty of protecting this compound soon wore off and the shifts could be quite mundane. However, the Flight also spent a lot of time on training weeks and honing our infantry skills. As the new lad I felt I had to prove myself and endeavoured to show I was a keen but good soldier. In time I was able to prove my worth and became a valued member of the Flight. Phil, one of the senior lads, took me under his wing and looked after me. I looked up to him and took in everything he taught me like a sponge; he was a seasoned gunner who knew a thing or two and I wanted to learn.

Regiment life was good and F Flight gelled as a really close unit with many opportunities to go out drinking together. Bury St Edmunds was our local town where most of the Regiment would descend upon on a Friday and Saturday night to get drunk. I even took on Phil's drinking attire of desert-boots, jeans and Hawaiian shirt with the shaved head which I now had taken to completely wet shaving. I was absorbing everything military life had to offer and I prided myself on being the tough soldier who didn't do emotions, I took to the drinking culture of Regiment life and the 'work-hard, play-hard' lifestyle. I was doing well in my career; my Sergeant and Corporals were impressed with my work effort and attitude and commented that I had what it takes to go far in the Regiment. For the first time in my life I felt that I was really living and had found what I was called to be. The Regiment was everything to me - it was now my very life, my very identity. Nothing would come between it and me.

Even though I was doing well as a young soldier and enjoyed every aspect of the life it had to offer, there were times I kept myself to myself, but at times I also wanted acceptance and belonging, even deep down to be truly loved by someone. In feeling this I would sometimes be submissive and try to be a 'people-pleaser' to get acceptance by my colleagues. Then, when advantage of my gentle nature had been taken, I would get angry at myself for allowing people to walk all over me. I would toughen up again and say no more. In my inner insecurity and lack of confidence and core belief, I felt unlovable and ugly. I struggled with chatting to girls on nights out. Trying to prove I was a tough hardened soldier on nights out, I would find myself fighting after a few drinks, whether it be with local civilians or American Air Force personnel from the local USAF base. Or it would be soldiers from the local army barracks. Fighting and drinking came with the territory of soldiering - or so we were led to believe. The golden rule was that you would always have your mate's back when out together, so fighting became all too common on nights out with the lads. Afterwards we would chat about our 'war stories' and who did what, and what happened to who, and so on. There were even times after a few too many drinks we would end up fighting with each other.

I did everything to extremes, whether it be my job or drinking. I would train physically to the extreme, always pushing myself to the limit and beyond, whether it was out running six miles or lifting weights in the gym. I always trained to be the best that I could be. I also had dreams of one day joining the ranks of the best, and desired to apply for Special Forces selection when I was ready. I loved my job, I loved my identity, I loved being physically strong and big and fit, I loved being a soldier. I started to go out with a girl who worked in the NAAFI (Navy Army and Air Force Institute), who provided the recreation, bars, cafes and shops on bases) and I thought I loved her. We went out for a few months and, in my naivety and lack of experience in relationships, I had this idea of marriage and kids, but this completely put her off, especially as she was still technically married and going through a messy divorce. Once, at home on leave on a night out with Steven, I met Kate and ended up having a drunken one night stand, but the next morning we swapped numbers and I headed back down to Honington. I confessed this to the girl I was seeing and was a bit taken aback to hear that she too had cheated on me at a point in our relationship. After chatting we amicably agreed to split up. I put this ended-relationship down to experience.

It was then that I arranged to head back up to Edinburgh on my next four days off to see Kate and, after spending a few days with her, we then entered into a relationship. This was the start of my regularly travelling to Scotland nearly every four days off, and the relationship became a long term one. For a while I didn't tell my parents that I was in Edinburgh; I knew mum wouldn't approve of me staying at Kate's and I didn't want the hassle. In time, as we established our relationship, I introduced Kate to my family. My family loved her and it meant a lot to me that they did. She was a loving woman who would do absolutely anything for me or anyone else; that was the type of person she was. I believed I had fallen in love with her. We had a great time together when I came home to see her and through Kate I made a lot of good friends and we had a great social life together, not just going out drinking, but hanging out at each other's places. I was also really enjoying my career in the Regiment; life seemed great. With the military came great opportunities to travel abroad and the summer of 1998 I got the opportunity to go to Holland with the Squadron to complete the Nijmegan March. It was a big event every year where teams or individuals, both military and civilian, would road march 100 miles in four days, completing 25 miles a day with a 25 pound bergen on our backs. It was a great week in Holland and an opportunity to have some serious drinking sessions with soldiers from other nations.

A few months after later opportunity called again, to go adventure training in Bavaria, Southern Germany. We certainly played hard and worked hard. In the evenings we would get totally wrecked in the local pubs and clubs, then by day we would be hitting it hard on the mountain treks or mountain biking into Austria, or kayaking in the local lakes. I came to pride myself on how much I could drink and still function the next day. In the military this was unofficially encouraged and there would be banter with those considered to be lightweights who couldn't keep up with everyone. Things were getting more serious with Kate and yet I was thinking how I could advance my career and leave the Squadron I was on for another.

The Regiment has No.2 Squadron, an airborne squadron who, like the Parachute Regiment, are parachute capable. They were considered by many in the Regiment the elite of the Corps, and many of us got into the airborne mentality. The only way to serve on this squadron as a fully integrated and accepted Gunner was to earn your parachute wings. The only way to do this was the complete the pre-para course and then complete the mandatory jumps at Brize Norton near Oxford. The pre-para consisted of a three-week physical course designed to push you to your limit and beyond, completing a series of fitness tests and speed marches with weight at certain times. It was both physically and mentally tough and hard to pass, with many people not passing first time around. I gave my complete focus and commitment to getting into the best shape possible; my only thought was to become airborne. I started the course with great ambition and determination to pass and was doing quite well until unfortunately, in the second week, on one of the hill speed marches I injured my knee and ended up coming off the course. I was pretty disheartened and hit the drink quite hard to drown my sorrows. After a week of recovery doing mundane duties at Squadron Headquarters I was put back on to full duties on my Flight. I thought about going for pre-para again in time, but for now got on with Regiment life and time with Kate in my time off.

Christmas came and went and it was in the new year of January 1999 that I really thought about my future, especially with Kate. I believed I truly loved her and wanted to spend my life with her, so I proposed and she delightfully accepted. Both our families couldn't have been happier and we planned to be married later that year. It was around this time I applied for a posting to No.3 Squadron based at RAF Aldergrove, Northern Ireland. I still had that dream to serve in the Province and this would be my ticket over there to and to get off the Squadron I was currently on. I had a few good mates in the Regiment, but I was particularly close to two lads called Jez and Flex, especially Flex. We were quite inseparable; we had gone through basic training together and served on the same Flight; we lived next door to each other in the block; we were even drinking buddies on our time off. He also applied for Northern Ireland and was posted out there before me. He was also getting married and it was an honour to be at his wedding with other Regiment brothers in our best blue uniforms. Flex and his new wife Sarah were like family to me. A few months after putting in for my posting great news came through saying that it had been granted and I would be sent out to the Province in early August; Flex arrived in the Province a month before me. With my own wedding to Kate set for September, my remaining weeks at Honington were filled with sorting all my kit out and preparing to go over the water to my new posting and a new chapter in my life and career. I really couldn't wait. I worked right up to the Friday I was due to head out, with the weekend in Edinburgh seeing Kate and my family before flying out on the Sunday of early August to start first thing Monday morning on 3 Squadron.

I flew to Belfast international Airport where I was met by one of my old corporals, who had been posted there before me, and he took me to camp and helped me settle in. I met the lads I would serve with and caught up with Flex and Sarah for a few drinks. After a week at Aldergrove I headed to Ballykinlar to do a Northern Ireland Reinforcement Training course to prepare me for serving on the streets of Belfast or whereever I would serve in the Province. After that, I joined B Flight and began operations with them. I took to the Squadron really quickly, not just the working regime but the social side as well. There were regular beer-calls in the Squadron bar on a Friday afternoon, if you were not on ops, and you were expected to be there as it was classed as a parade. They knew I was due to be married in a few weeks and at one beer call on a typical Friday, B Flight threw a stag-party on me when I least expected it. I was to dress in a frock, handcuffed inside a wheelie bin and then wheeled to all the bars on camp. It certainly was a work-hard, play-hard culture. I out-drank a lot of the guys and was one of the few still standing at the end of the night. I just loved my job and every aspect of it. I went home on leave and got married to Kate and together we came back to the Province, excited for our new life that was about to begin.

It took us a few weeks to be allocated a married quarter on base, so I stayed on camp while Kate stayed with her dad, who lived only a few miles away from the base. I was given a few hours off to move into our new quarter and I was then back to work while Kate set up home and got everything how she wanted it. Kate had got a transfer with her work so she would be working in Belfast city during the week. On our first weekend we went down to the squadron bar for a few drinks with the lads and their wives and had a good night, with opportunity for Kate to meet the other wives. Life was brilliant; I had a job I loved, a wife who loved me and a career ahead of me. The honeymoon period and romance of how life was at this time was short-lived and the reality of how hard it was to be a working couple living in Northern Ireland would soon hit us. I say this because I put my job first and foremost, even before my marriage and when the demands of my marriage were to clash with the priority of my job, that was when problems arose. Furthermore, Kate was not and would never be a typical 'forces wife'. She was independent, driven, had a career of her own and wouldn't bow down to the expectations and the demands that came with being the wife of a serving soldier.

Kate's work pattern and my operational commitments resulted in our time available together becoming less and less. It didn't help that Kate would tell people in her office what I did for a living and I didn't know who they were or their background. She would go on work nights out in bars that were out of bounds to me as a serviceman, because of the security situation in Northern Ireland. Kate really didn't socialise with the other Squadron wives and started putting demands on me about what time she wanted me back home when I went out with the lads on camp or attended the beer calls which were classed as squadron parades. Putting demands on me made me rebel even more and I would selfishly come home when I wanted to. I liked a drink a bit too much and was one of those who, after having a few, did not want to stop drinking and would carry drinking until being physically kicked out of the bar at closing time.

Due to my shift patterns and Kate's work in Belfast, we would hardly see each other all week. Whole days at a time could go by before we saw each other and even then, we would be like passing ships. This would be our pattern of life for some time, feeling as if we were both living independent lives and just sharing the same house and bed. She had a social life off camp which I was not part of, and I had my time with the lads as well, drinking and socialising. When out drinking with the lads we use to joke that if we were meant to have a wife, then we would go to stores and be issued with one. I selfishly put my career as a soldier first, above everything, even my marriage. I put going out drinking with the guys as more important than spending time with Kate. I started to resent Kate's requests for me to spend time with her and show her attention - it became a problem if it interfered with drinking with the guys or time at work. I was being completely unfair, but I didn't let that register. Another problem I also seemed to let develop was to get angry at myself for compromising who I was in trying to fit in with the 'in' crowd on the Flight. Trying to be accepted by a certain corporal and trying to please him - for what? So I could be in his little clique? That's when I would get angry at myself, for allowing people to walk all over me and I would start telling myself to get a grip and harden up again. Deep down I just wanted acceptance and approval and was looking for it in all the wrong places and all the wrong people. I just didn't see it at the time.

Around August 2000 it all kicked off in the Shankill area of West Belfast, which was the Protestant heartland of Belfast. The Ulster Freedom Fighters (UFF) and the Ulster Volunteer Force (UVF) had started a turf war, and between them they had carried out numerous killings on both sides. Along with the army and in support of the Royal Ulster Constabulary (RUC) we were also deployed to the streets of West Belfast to try and bring normality and stability back to the area. We were deployed for around 6 weeks supporting the RUC to bring control back to the streets. On one of the first nights we were deployed just off the Crumlin Road carrying out Vehicle Checkpoints (VCPs) when we heard gunshots coming from a few streets away. Later the next morning we discovered that a UFF member had come out of the housing estate just around the corner from us, and emptied his pistol into a parked car that had members of the UVF in it. In less than a minute the man responsible had disappeared back into the housing estate before he could be apprehended.

A particular incident that comes to mind was when we were again carrying out VCPs just off Carlisle Circus Roundabout, which was just off the Crumlin Road. We had allowed a young lad no older than around six to stand on the bonnet of the 'Snatch' Land-Rover. This young lad asked me a question, saying "Oi mister are you a Prod or a Catholic?". I answered him "I'm a Prod of course why do you ask?". The young lad then replied; "Just checking mister." He then asked; "Can I borrow your gun mister?" I responded "Why do you want to borrow my gun?" Then the young lad answered "So I can go over that peace line and shoot one of those Catholics." I was certainly taken aback by his answer but started laughing. As look back now it makes me realise what hope was there for the youth when the bigotry and hatred was inbred into them at such a young age. If that lad had been born a hundred yards down the road on the Catholic divide, then he would have had the same hatred instilled into him against the Protestants.

I really enjoyed my time on the streets of West Belfast and working with the RUC. Another aspect of our job was constantly conducting public order training alongside the RUC and with the army, in case we ever had to be deployed and deal with riots. We had a few interesting clashes with the army on training exercises when the army were playing the rioters. A few fights nearly broke out between us. Not long after being deployed to the streets of West Belfast, B Flight 3 Squadron was then deployed to South Armagh and Armagh City. It was certainly an eventful and exciting time down there. When I came back from one of the detachments to South Armagh things were to take a turn for me.

Kate was away for the weekend in Edinburgh and I had gone out with the lads on camp that night when we got back from Armagh. I decided to throw a party at our quarter and had loads of lads around, drinking till the early hours. After everyone had left, I went online and got chatting to a girl from Belfast in an internet chat room. Not thinking properly, I arranged to meet her the next day in the city for a coffee (I certainly wasn't thinking here, or being fair to my wife. I was only thinking of myself.) We met and I was totally smitten by her and I arranged to meet her that night in a club near camp. That night a whole load of us went out to the club and I met her there and was really taken with her. The next day I thought about my life and selfishly decided I was missing out and that I was trapped in a marriage I didn't want to be in, I was even questioning did I even really love Kate. My thoughts were that I wanted to just have fun and be single again.

After I picked Kate up from the airport and got home, I became so cold and selfish towards her. I just came right out with it and told her what I was thinking and how I was missing out and wanted to be single again, even saying that I truly didn't know if I loved her anymore and felt trapped. To say I hurt her and how much I was breaking her heart was an understatement. That night I moved back into the block and our marriage was in tatters. Like I said my job came first, above my marriage. I was to start on a slippery slope. I started to see this girl from Belfast but did not get her cleared by the intelligence section, which in time was to get me into trouble. My mental state started to suffer as I tried to cope with everything that was going on. I started to go off the rails in my thinking, my actions and my decisions. Lads I worked with started to notice a change in me and this was being commented on.

Things came to a head when, after an all-day drinking session, I made a complete idiotic, irrational and reckless decision. I took the car without Kate knowing and decided I had enough I was going to run off and join the Foreign Legion. I ended up crashing into a car in the car park of a nightclub that I stopped at for a drink. After literally knocking my out through the car window in a rage, the guy whose car I had hit saw that I was completely drunk and drove me back to camp saying that if I would admit fault and we claim it on the insurance, no further action would be taken by him and the police would not be involved. The the help of my Regiment seniors that got me out this mess, as they covered for me and I got away with drink driving. I was looked after by my Sgt and I was very, very lucky.

Due to my irrational behaviour I went to see the doctor. Because of the stress that he sensed I was going through, he downgraded me temporarily from operational duties. The car was recovered the next day and thankfully fixed on the insurance, but without question, I was putting Kate through emotional turmoil. Shamefully, I wasn't really caring too much at this point, because all I could think of was my own inner turmoil. I was then put under investigation due to my recent actions and behaviour. it came known that I was seeing Sarah from West Belfast, without having her cleared with a security background check through the intelligence section. I was to come under military law and be punished for breaking the strict out of bounds rule in place. While reflecting on everything that had recently happened, I truly believed I had fallen in love with Sarah and in all this mess, it was Sarah I wanted to be with.

I was marched into my Commanding Officer and read the charge of breaking the strict out of bounds brief. I was awarded a £200 fine and an official warning should I choose to accept this. I was lucky and gladly accepted it; it could have been a lot worse and ended my career. The consequences of my actions meant that I was to lose the opportunity of promotion by a few years. My annual assessment was affected and I lost the recommendation for promotion that I had had previously. I got off very lightly, but my thought was 'I still have my career', which was the only thing I truly held onto. I promised myself to never get in this situation again. It was evident that the Regiment certainly looked after their own. I now started to try and put my life back together and get on with life. Kate was to move back to Edinburgh just before Christmas. I did what I could to help her move out of the quarter and head home. She was very emotional and upset the day she left. I couldn't blame her in the slightest as I had totally destroyed the life she believed she had. It felt so strange, being left with an empty married quarter to get in order to hand back, and I felt a weight had been lifted when I signed it back over to the accommodation department. I gained clearance for Sarah so we could see each other and made plans to get on with my career and back to operational duties.

After Christmas I managed to get upgraded back to operational status and my career was starting to get back on track. Life was going well, I was working hard and enjoying my time with Sarah. But I was to throw it all down the pan by getting involved with a girl in Edinburgh on leave after a drunken night out, which led to lies and excuses and inevitably, Sarah and me splitting up. I believed the job came first and threw away the relationship I had with Sarah, After our break-up I realised the huge regret I had for what I had thrown away; I carried this deep regret for a long time and couldn't believe what a fool I had been. After our break-up and as time went on, I realised how much I loved

Sarah, a love that I carried deep inside for a long, long time. I got on with life on the Squadron, proving myself again as a trustworthy and reliable soldier. I did what I only knew best and that was to be a soldier, but I was drinking heavily at the weekends and also getting into fights with the army lads at the regular weekend discos on base.

I was still speaking to Sarah on the 'phone from time to time. I think neither of us could pluck up the courage to tell each other we still loved each other. Sarah would ring me out of the blue, but I hated myself for the fact I didn't fight to win her back. I put my career first, but deep down I wanted to be loved with someone that loved me, but in my own pain I pushed my emotions deep, as I was this tough man that I kept trying to be. A few months later Kate came over to see her dad and we arranged to meet up. Seeing her stirred up feelings that made me think that there was still a love there for her. After time together we somehow agreed to maybe trying again and see what it would lead to. For the coming weeks things seemed to have taken a turn and going well. Kate and I seemed to be doing well and it looked as if our marriage could be salvaged. I had proved my worth again on my Flight and we were very busy on operations serving all around the border towns of South Armagh. With local elections in place around the province, we were deployed with the RUC to provide security for the voting process and ensure that no terrorist incidents hindered the election. I had my third-year application to stay in Northern Ireland approved, life seemed back on track, I was living life, I was loving my job, but my heart ached for Sarah, but I let her go upon hearing that she was back with her ex.

I was still drinking to excess at the weekends and enjoying the attention I was getting in the bars. This led me to cheating on Kate with a one-night stand; my thinking being that we weren't officially back together yet- I was in the

Province and Kate was in Edinburgh. Early one Saturday morning, after a drinking session, not thinking I took a gamble and I got a taxi to Sarah's in West Belfast, in my drunken hope to win her back. But to my surprise, her ex stuck his head out of the top window when I rang the bell. I was able to think quickly and shouted up as if I had pressed the wrong door-bell and was wanting next door. He shouted down 'no problem' and was none the wiser as to who I was, but I knew exactly who he was. After heading to Belfast City and getting a coffee and coming to my senses, I realised how idiotic I had been. If I had got caught being somewhere that was out of bounds my career would have been well and truly over. That summer of 2001 saw an opportunity; a second chance to start a fresh with Kate.

A short-notice posting came for me to be posted to newly reformed No.51 Squadron, who were now based at RAF Lossiemouth, near Elgin in Morayshire, Scotland. This was just what we needed, and Kate wanted, as there were too many bad memories for Catherine to want to return to Aldergrove. After a few phone calls and paperwork signed, my posting of three years to Northern Ireland was back to two, which meant that I could accept the posting and soon be off to Lossiemouth. But I wasn't truly fair though; deep down I still held a torch and a hope for Sarah. This was truly selfish on my part as I was not being totally honest with Kate. On my last day at Aldergrove I reached out to Sarah by phoning and texting her to say I was due to fly out that day from Belfast City Airport. I asked her to meet me before I flew and that I wanted to see her. I waited anxiously at the airport in the hope she would come. Knowing if she had I would have selfishly hurt Kate again and thrown away any chance of a reconciliation in the hope for a future with Sarah. Gutted I waited until the very last minute, but had to board the flight for Edinburgh. In my heart I realised that this chapter of my life was now closed and so I

headed back to Scotland to make a supposedly
"Fresh Start."

Chapter 4

A couple weeks leave at home in Edinburgh seemed like bliss, having believed I had now put Northern Ireland behind me. I focussed on making this fresh start work and looked forward to getting up to Lossiemouth and getting started. I drove up early on a Monday morning heading up to Lossiemouth to start my new life on 51 Squadron. While home on leave we decided that Kate would stay in Edinburgh due to her career and the flat we owned (well, Kate really owned) and I would stay at Lossiemouth during the week and commute home at the weekends. I actually quite liked the idea of this set-up as it meant, for me, that I would have a life up north and a family life at the weekends Again, I was really thinking about myself and my career.

I settled in very quickly and really enjoyed being on the Squadron, I especially enjoyed Lossiemouth's location, its beautiful beaches, great pubs and the locals who were so friendly and welcoming. I loved the fact that we were the only Regiment squadron based there, so we were quite a novelty factor; the other RAF trades were wary of us and we certainly were not short of female attention and admiration. All the lads on the squadron bonded very quickly and we became a tight unit that had each other's backs; we were certainly a force to be reckoned with in any fights during nights out with the locals or even other RAF serviceman. We were "Rockapes" and we lived up to the reputation that Regiment Gunners had for drinking, fighting and womanising.

For me, being at Lossiemouth during the week and then heading home for weekends in Edinburgh was like the icing on the cake. I felt that it couldn't get any better than this. In my heart I really tried to make a go of it with Kate. Trying to be the hard-working soldier during the week and the faithful committed husband when home; for me though, the military still came first. Everything seemed to be going smoothly with the current setup. I was doing well on the Squadron, earning the trust and respect of my seniors. I had made a few close friends and was bonding well with all the other lads. I was proving myself as a soldier and was selected as a section 2i/c (Fire Team Commander). I got on great with my Corporal, Frank, who lived opposite me in the block, and I introduced him to Kate's best friend (they both went on to marry and have kids). The Squadron were only at half manning level at this point and made up of 2 flights, A and B flight. These were training and preparing to deploy to Kuwait as part of the rotational Field Squadron carrying out operations at Ali Al Salem Airbase; protecting the base as part of enforcing the no fly zone over Iraq.

One otherwise normal weekend, heading home to celebrate Kate's 30th birthday, things took a twist. It was the weekend that I introduced Frank to his wife-to-be. We were heading to

Edinburgh in the car and I got a missed call from a number I knew too well. After stopping for a quick lunch-break, I proceeded to phone the number back. It was Sarah's number and although her calling had surprised me, I was also quite happy that she did. Sarah went on to tell me that she had just had a miscarriage. In my selfishness and denial, I asked if it was with the boyfriend that she had got back together with. Sarah said it was. We small talked for a few minutes and then I was back on the road. What I wasn't realising at the time was that Sarah was trying to reach out to me in her pain and loss. But I was too selfish and didn't want anything to ruin how things were going for me at the time, especially as my career was starting to blossom with promotion on the cards if I kept doing what I was doing. I was not prepared to let anyone come in between. But as I was driving, Sarah was on my mind - and was for a very long time after that. The weekend came and went and we celebrated Kate's 30th at a venue in Edinburgh. But where was I during the whole celebration? Where you would always find me when I went out; propping up the bar, getting drunk. This was me at my worst, not being fair or honest with Kate and only thinking of myself and my career.

Life on the Squadron went on as normal, busy with exercises and training for Kuwait. I carried on, getting drunk with the lads during the week and going home at the weekends. On a routine deployment to Garelochead to carry out exercises and live firing ranges, everything was about to change. It was 11th September 2001 and I had just come off a pairs fire and manoeuvre range with Mac when someone dropped the bombshell; "You're not got gonna believe - this some numpties have flown planes into the World Trade Centre." "Yeah right good one, you're pulling my leg," was my response. But he wasn't kidding and as we listened on the radio to what was unfolding, different thoughts were going through our minds. We thought that this meant war and we were excited at the prospect.

The rest of the day and following days were quite surreal. That night security on camp went up to the highest level and I found myself on guard duty. We were continually briefed on security updates but eventually finished our field firing and exercises and went back to Lossiemouth. In the coming weeks we had daily briefings and intelligence reports; we were still heading to Kuwait as planned but operational commitments and intentions stepped up as the world adapted to what had happened on September 11th. Our outline of exercises and training targets changed considerably. We deployed to Machrahanish for specific operational training before deploying to Kuwait in December. Life carried on at a fast pace and soon it came for us to deploy to Kuwait for our first tour there. I was raring to go and couldn't wait to get there.

In Early December of 2001 the Squadron deployed a contingent of troops to Kuwait to take over ground protection of Ali Al Salem Airbase. Our role would be to protect the base from the southern sector while the United States Air Force Security Police protected the northern sector. Our role included vehicle patrols of four-man fire teams, in stripped-down Land Rovers, patrolling anywhere up to 6 miles from the base.

We provided protection for a prototype Nuclear Biological and Chemical (NBC) warfare unit that was deployed north of the air base whose role was to give early indication of any chemical threat launched by Saddam Hussein. The air base was divided into sectors with contingents from different nations there, all to support the operation of the no fly-zone over Iraq. When we had down time, we could use the American facilities on base or one of the recreational facilities in Kuwait City, or we would be able to head into the City and use the hotels or shopping centres.

Each morning all the team commanders received a briefing, going over the recent patrols and intelligence reports for any potential threat, locally or potentially from Iraq itself. Even though there was a potential threat it was an enjoyable tour. I was responsible as a team commander for a four-man Fire Team, but regularly we would work as an eight-man Section with my Section Corporal in charge. I really enjoyed the patrols in the desert, especially the night patrols, and the freedom we felt we had in where we were able to patrol.

I was close with my Fire Team and off duty we would hang out together in Kuwait itself either at one of the hotel pools, or shopping in the local markets. I was focussed; I was very professional in my role and I took leading my Fire Team very seriously, especially with the tasks we were given. I was being noticed by my seniors and it was being commented on the bright future I had in the Regiment. I was really enjoying my time in Kuwait and to me my job was everything.

The first tour went by pretty uneventfully and, after a time at home on leave, my Section were kept in the UK for the last six weeks of the tour. The remaining few of us at Lossiemouth were selected to go to Bisley, to represent the Squadron at the Annual RAF Regiment Shooting Competition. For me, with idle time on my hands, I started to drink heavily again, enjoying all the opportunities to drink when away from the shooting. I started flirting with local girls and was unfaithful. I was living by the old-school 'what happens on tour stays on tour' mentality. I wasn't the only married man being unfaithful, but it wasn't an excuse. I was having my cake and eating it. To me, this was an opportunity to have some fun.

We came back from the shooting competition and life was pretty boring with only a few of us at the Squadron hangar each day. When I wasn't training hard during the week, I was out drinking in Lossiemouth and being unfaithful there. I enjoyed the attention and shamefully would go home at the weekends and pretend to be the doting husband. I was burning the candle at both ends and it would only be a matter of time before the wick burned out. A few of us were selected to go and shoot in the RAF Annual Shooting Competition and again it was back to Bisley. For me, it was another week of drinking, flirting and cavorting; I certainly wasn't thinking of anyone but myself over this time.

The Squadron finally came back from the first tour and there was a medal presentation for all the lads that had served. Because I already had the General Service Medal with Northern Ireland clasp, I was awarded another clasp to go on my medal with Air Operations Iraq on it. I felt proud to have my number one uniform on and be awarded the second clasp. I look back now and if only my behaviour and actions had matched the picture of the immaculate soldier, standing on parade with a medal on his chest. Oh, how a uniform can give a false image of someone and who they truly are.

That summer we were busy preparing for our second tour in Kuwait; we were only going to be home for four months and then we would deploy again. I really couldn't wait. Between busy periods of training for Kuwait that summer, if we weren't away on exercise or courses we would be at Lossiemouth and getting wrecked. I was drinking when I could and being unfaithful with someone local. Kate and I moved from the flat to a house we had bought together We went on holiday to Mexico where my drinking got completely out of control and I put myself in some very risky situations.

It wasn't long before we were only about two weeks away from deploying back to Kuwait for our second tour. Some of the seniors were looking for volunteers who would do the whole four-month tour and without hesitation I put my hand up. This got noticed and my thinking was how this would help with promotion prospects. It certainly impressed my seniors of my commitment and loyalty to the Regiment. The one thing I wasn't thinking of was my wife; the fact that my marriage was now built on deceit and lies, with my selfish thinking that she would be none the wiser. I lied to Kate and told her It was mandatory that I was going for the full four months. As I have said I put my job first and my marriage second, I only thought about myself. Because I had volunteered, I was put in charge of the Headquarters Fire Team which meant more administration work in Kuwait but a real opportunity to impress the more senior officers and advance my career further. So, time came again, we were back in our desert fatigues and heading back to Kuwait via Cyprus. I thought the day wouldn't come soon enough and was excited the day we boarded the Hercules to fly out. I was again finally on my way back to Kuwait.

Back at Ali Al Salem there was a different atmosphere now; things were very different, there was a sense of a more urgency. Things had now escalated in the Middle East and there was ever more political pressure being put on Saddam Hussein and especially in light of his supposed weapons of mass destruction. They weren't telling people back home but the coalition were preparing for a war. Out in the desert, near where the prototype NBC unit was deployed, two mass tent cities had appeared of nowhere literally overnight. The Americans were pouring troops into these new tent cities. Each day, convoys went past Ali Al Salem Airbase bringing machinery, weaponry and troops into the desert. There was an army building and they were preparing; war was coming. The daily intelligence briefs we were getting informed us of the escalating situation that was developing with Iraq and the threat they were presenting.

Even though I was the HQ Fire Team commander, busy with more administration work than actual patrols, life it had its perks. It meant that I worked a 9-to-5 day, with use of any of the HQ vehicles; it meant I had time to seriously train in the gym and opportunities to really impress my bosses. But to be honest the work could get mundane and boring at times, with duties like refuelling all the vehicles. or making sure all the radio batteries were charged. I missed being on the regular patrols outside the wire. I was very close with Dougie, my Flight Sergeant at the time and was discussing with him the potential of going for Special Forces selection. He really encouraged me to think seriously about going for it. This was when I really got serious about my fitness training and was pushing myself to get in shape for selection. I would be going for 'bergen runs' around the airfield at 9 o clock at night, in the dark. I was that serious to really get myself focussed. Dougie even helped me to learn about military knowledge beyond my level which would help me succeed. However, something was to unfold that was to make me question everything about myself.

One afternoon I had a missed call on my phone. The number was showing this time and, to my surprise, bringing the number up showed that it was Sarah. As we spoke, I jokingly said "have you rung me to tell me, you still love me?". I did not expect her to say yes, but that was not the main reason she called. I knew without question, without her having to say another word, what she was phoning about. I knew it was about the baby she had miscarried the year before. I said to her that the baby was mine wasn't it? At that she said yes, it was. As we talked she explained that she tried to tell me last time we spoke but had lost the confidence.

Sarah explained that she didn't want to ruin my trying with Kate again, she didn't know how to tell me and didn't want to hurt me. We spoke more and more and I found out that she knew she was pregnant before we split up but couldn't tell me, because if I had known I would never have got back with Kate and I would never have left Northern Ireland; I would never have left her on her own. Sarah went on to tell me it was a wee girl and she called her Sarah too. I asked her what she would have called the baby if it had been a boy. She said she would have called him Bruce after his daddy. Hearing that made me choke with emotion.

We chatted some more, and I managed to say to her that I still loved her and had never stopped loving her, at which she told me she still loved me too. After the conversation I wrote her a letter, spilling my heart into it, but inevitably she never replied. We spoke a couple more times but after that I could not get hold of her again. After the initial phone call my head was all over the place in trying to process what had just happened and what I now knew. It wasn't until that evening, as I was having a chat with Lynn, a Reservist attached to the Squadron, that out of the blue I completely broke down. I sobbed my heart out like a little boy. I was grieving the loss of this precious little daughter I never got to meet or know; a little girl that would have been the best thing ever to happen to me and who I would have loved unconditionally but that was taken from me. My emotions were all over the place. I was angry, hurting, broken and confused with all manner of emotions pouring out of me. First and foremost, I was angry at God. I blamed Him for taking away my daughter. I was angry and bitter towards Sarah for knowing and not telling me, but at the same time yearning for her and feeling helpless for not being there for her in her moment of grief and loss.

I started to think all manner of irrational things; if only I had been there for her and had never left Northern Ireland, my daughter would be here (as if I could have made a difference). I felt guilt for not reaching out her when she initially tried to tell me and was reaching out to me in her loss and pain. I was too selfish at that time to take responsibility that the baby was mine but instead asked her if it was her ex's. How I hated myself right now, but the news of the baby being mine emotionally broke me. It made me question everything and I was struggling to process it all. I went to see Dougie and confided to him what had happened, struggling not to break down. He was brilliant and gave me 24 hours off to try and get my head sorted. I felt completely numb inside trying to make sense of things, and that's when I decided to get my head back in the game. I hardened my heart and pushed my emotions and feelings deep down. I made a vow to myself that I would never let anyone get close or hurt me again.

Things were heating up in Kuwait with the build-up of troops and potential of war. I got myself together and focussed back on my job. I spoke with my Flight Sergeant and managed to get moved back to a patrolling Fire Team, as a team commander; the rest of the squadron had been recalled to Kuwait as the operational

manning level went up. During my time on that
the second tour, a couple of interesting
situations unfolded. One in particular was on a
routine patrol driving through the desert when,
out of nowhere, an American Cobra helicopter
appeared, hovering straight in front of us. We
stopped suddenly, and for what seemed like the
longest 30 seconds, we all looked at each other
and then at the helicopter, not sure if they were
going to open fire on us. On return to base, I
reported this incident to my seniors at morning
briefings and my Commanding Officer went
ballistic, he was straight on the phone to the
Americans.

Another incident could also have turned into a
'blue-on-blue' with the Americans. In the early
hours, on a night patrol, we spotted soldiers
parachuting into our area of responsibility. We
approached with caution ready to engage if
necessary. Thankfully, they were American
Special Forces carrying out a training jump in
full kit. Unfortunately, they had failed to inform

our Operations Room of their training jump. Once again, my CO was going ballistic on the phone to the Americans.

As we were approaching Christmas and due to return home, the atmosphere was tense at Ali Al Salem. From the intelligence briefs we had been getting, we knew we would be back out in Kuwait again in the New Year. The threat of war was imminent and the coalition were preparing seriously for it, yet back home the general public did not know half of what was going on out there and the preparations for war. Things moved very fast there, and we had been busy, getting ready for what was coming. It was nice to be heading home for Christmas, but my head and my heart were centred on returning to Kuwait in the New Year. I was getting myself focussed and ready for a war.

Chapter 5

Even though I was physically at home that Christmas, my mind was elsewhere. It was thinking about our return to Kuwait and what would be the coming situation with Iraq. I had suppressed everything about Sarah and the loss of my daughter. I did not want to think about it and knew I could not speak to Kate about it. My heart was far from Kate and in a place of confusion, not knowing where it truly belonged. After Christmas leave, back at the Squadron preparing for our return to Kuwait. everyone was busy either on courses or training, preparing for our deployment. In my downtime I got drunk in the local bars of Lossiemouth. In early February of 2003, after a few days leave, the orders came in and we were finally to head back out to the Middle East. Saying goodbye to Kate was quite surreal - it had not truly hit home that I didn't know when would be the next time that I would see her.

The Squadron travelled by coach to RAF Uxbridge, south-west of London, it being a pre holding area before an eventual deployment to Kuwait. Unfortunately, we had to travel in civilian clothing in case we offended someone on the way. This political correctness irritated us; we were about to go to war and I for one wanted nothing more than to be able to wear my uniform with pride. We were to stay at Uxbridge until further notice, so we did what many a soldier would do; we went into Uxbridge to get drunk, realising that some of us may not come home. After a few days the Squadron were moved to a central processing area, where all troops deploying to Kuwait underwent administration and were processed to deploy; we experienced the usual military "hurry up and wait" game. Eventually the Squadron moved to RAF Brize Norton and we flew to Kuwait City, where we were then bussed to Ali Al Salem Air Base. Again, the "hurry up and wait" game was played as we were allocated accommodation. It seemed strange to be back in Kuwait after such a short time; if anything it felt as if we hadn't even left the country. Ali Al Salem had become a thriving, busy place.

A variety of encampments had been built all around the airfield. Many contingents were here, from the British army and the RAF, to US Marine Corps (USMC), US Army and US Air Force (USAF), all busy with their own operations to get combat ready. We spent the next few weeks getting acclimatised, fitness training, weapons training and stripping-down our Land Rovers when they arrived in port. The Squadron also moved to different encampment on the air-base, where we settled down until our deployment. As the next few weeks went by, and the deadline for Saddam to comply with the sanctions against him drew nearer and nearer, war was becoming more certain. It was then that we were to be briefed on what our role would be should we go to war. The Squadron was called in by our Commanding Officer to give us orders and the outline of 51 Squadron RAF Regiment's role.

We had been tasked with crossing the Kuwait/Iraq border from the south to take and hold Safwan airstrip while the USMC 5 Light Armoured Reconnaissance Regiment would sweep to the left around Jebel Sanam and come in from the north. Jebel Sanam was the only key high ground that overlooked the airstrip and surrounding area. The plan was first to pound the Jebel by Cobra helicopters the night before, followed by a helicopter assault from Marine Force Recon. They would take the Jebel and, once secured, leave a RAF Regiment sniper team in place to oversee and give cover as we crossed over the border to take Safwan Airstrip. The mission was to take the airstrip, secure it, then hold it so that it could be used as a launch-pad to push further into Iraq. The airstrip would become what we call a Forward Arming and Refuelling Point, or FARP. An interesting fact about Safwan Airstrip was that it had been used in 1991 for the surrender and signing of surrender papers by the Iraqi generals during the previous Gulf war.

So, we had our mission and we knew what our role would be; this was when we started getting focussed in our training for what was to come. I was made up to Acting Corporal and I would be leading an eight-man section over the border, as my Corporal had been relocated to the sniper team that was to go in with Marine Force Recon. We kitted-out and customised the Land Rovers for the job ahead. We carried out exercise after exercise in the desert, getting SOPs (Standard Operating Procedures) squared away, anticipating all potential situations. We carried out contact drills after contact drills until we could do them without thinking. When we weren't training, we had some down-time in the evenings on camp. In the huge recreation tent I would shave some of the lads' heads for them. As so many people were wanting shaved heads I became the unofficial camp barber - I could have made a fortune if I had charged everyone! I even had to shave the Squadron Warrant Officer's head. Woe-betide if I messed up his haircut, as the Warrant Officer was a feisty Scotsman who you did not want to get on the wrong side of.

Our Squadron was only still half-squadron size, so our numbers were bolstered by the Queen's Colour Squadron (QCS) the RAF's Ceremonial Squadron who, on operational duties, were No.63 Squadron RAF Regiment, but here fell under 51 Squadron's banner. These guys were needed and we very much appreciated having them alongside us as we became a full squadron. As time progressed and with war looming, the training and briefings intensified, and we spent a lot of time training in the desert alongside our Marine counterparts. I recall one particularly funny incident when this huge, muscle-bound African-American U.S Marine came, asking for one of our ration packs and what could he swap for it. It seemed that our

MREs (Meals Ready to Eat) as he called them were so much better than theirs, as ours contained more than the US versions. Apparently, he had eaten 3 of our ration packs already. What he didn't realise was that one of our ration packs was designed for a 24 hour period, not just for one sitting as theirs were!

In those last few days at Ali Al Salem Air Base before we moved up to the Border, with time getting ever nearer to war being declared, things started to get pretty intense, but exciting and surreal at the same time. I remember so well the issuing of ammunition, grenades, morphine, anti-tank weapons and getting our final orders before we moved out; phoning home on our last night on camp and speaking to Kate, my sister and my parents, not knowing when or if I would speak to them again. Like many soldiers that night, I was alone with my thoughts, thinking "this is it - this is for real - we are going to war". I was caught up with a mixture of feelings and emotions; excitement, apprehension, fear and so many more. I wouldn't be honest if I didn't say that I thought and worried 'what if I got killed'. For the first time, I truly felt a sense of fear come upon me before I suppressed everything. I remember actually getting down onto one knee, closing my eyes and calling out to God, fearful. I spoke out to Him and asked "God will you get me through this and get me home."

Our last day at Ali Al Salem was a day of anticipation and excitement. The whole Squadron was assembled together for a group photo, and then loaded onto our vehicles and headed out in convoy, while one of the gunners played the bagpipes. We closed to near the Iraq border and deployed into a waiting area for the deadline to come. We were only there a few hours when we moved up to our final position. As we were moving by tactical convoy at night, we could see in the distance, over the border, the oilfields being set on fire. In the early hours we were in our final position and started to dig shell scrapes next to our vehicles and settle in and try and get some sleep. We deployed camouflage netting over the vehicles and got into routine, playing the 'hurry up and wait' game again as the deadline for Saddam was only a few hours away.

During the day, alarms occasionally sounded for potential chemical attack. On one occasion, I was a few hundred yards from the vehicles, having taken a spade to go about my business. The alarm sounded during that process. The lads were laughing as I quickly tried to get myself in order, put on my respirator at the same time and run back to my team's position. Thankfully I had no mishap. The deadline came and went, and we were briefed that war had been declared. I think all of us were especially excited; weeks of waiting, build-up and frustration had finally come to a head. We were at war, we were finally going to do this for real. As darkness fell, we first heard and then saw them; two American Cobra helicopters, followed by 2 more, flying low over us. A lot of us cheered and shouted to 'go get them' and a few more choice words. Jebel Sanam was just ahead of us and we watched as the first strike of the war took place. The Cobra helicopters opened fire and unleashed what looked like Hell onto the Jebel – intelligence had reported there was a military outpost on top of the Jebel. The ground shook under us and nothing like the movies could compare to what we were seeing and experiencing before our very eyes. We watched through the night as Cobra helicopters were flying over us taking the fight to the enemy. The ground was constantly shaking under us as war was underway.

Not many of us slept much that night, the adrenaline was keeping us awake. The next morning the team commanders, including myself, received a briefing with an update of intelligence on what had happened so far. We learned the USMC had obliterated the Jebel. Marine Force Recon had taken the Jebel, secured it and were moving forward, while our Regiment sniper team were in situation and were now providing watch from the high ground for our crossing. We were briefed that the Royal Marines had launched an offensive at the port of Um Quasar and had taken ground. We also learned of the first casualties from our side. A helicopter with Royal Marines and a journalist on board had gone down with everyone killed. But we were ready for casualties, it was part of war. We were briefed to take down all our camouflage netting and fill in our shell scrapes and be ready to move at a moment's notice.

We were in position most of the day and that night we moved out to our final rendezvous, right at the border where we would launch over into Iraq at first light.

In our final briefing there were reports that we would be facing a battalion of republican guard and to expect casualties when we crossed the border. I was on high alert and the adrenaline was working overtime. I kept going over in my head what my role was as a section commander, what my orders were and everything we had been training for. I didn't sleep very much in the few hours we had. Then came the orders to kit up, mount up and prepare to move. This was it - we were going over. Everything we had trained for had come to this point. Our war was about to begin. I was on high alert, buzzing off the adrenaline, ready to go. We were immensely proud that, apart from the Royal Marines entering Iraq through the port from the sea, we were actually to be the first British troops to cross the border by land. As dawn started to surface, we were on the move and crossing the border. This was it - I was ready, I wanted a fight. I wanted to kill, I wanted action, I was ready to die in battle if it came to that. We were swiftly across the border, and at speed moved with purpose into the positions tactically around the airstrip, deploying into all-round defence waiting for the attack. Frustratingly, it never came. The enemy we were expecting had run off through the night, before a fight could take place. I was so frustrated at this, but training took over and I got my section prepared for the next phase of operation.

My section was to carry out a clearance patrol to the west of Safwan airstrip while the EOD (bomb disposal) boys were tasked with clearing Safwan airstrip itself so that it would be operational for helicopters to land. My section was to search any dwellings within the area of the airstrip for any weapons locals might have and clear the area of any potential threat. Once I briefed the lads exactly what our orders were and what we were tasked to do, we mounted up and headed out to carry out a clearance patrol. Not even five minutes into the patrol we spotted a huge 1,000-pound unexploded ordnance at the side of the tracked road. It was from one of our aircraft. As we stopped to mark its position, a Land Rover came toward us and it so happened to be engineers from the EOD team that came across the border with us. I liaised with the commander of the vehicle and showed him where the thousand pounder was so that he could deal with it. I remember his face and that of the driver so well. They are imprinted on my mind, because we were to find out that they were ambushed and killed en-route to Ramallah only a few hours later. It was hard to believe they were killed and I had seen them only a few hours earlier.

We carried out our patrol without drama, searching people's buildings on our patrol for weapons and coming across none. The locals we met seemed friendly enough and pleased to see us. After our patrol, we reported back to the foot of the Jebel and were tasked with carrying out vehicle check points (VPs) on the track coming in from the north. We worked in four-man teams on rotation in order to get into a routine, get fed and have some rest. My Flight Commander called me for orders before last light and I was briefed that my section was to set up an observation post (OP) on the south west side of the Jebel, watching for any possible threat coming from that direction. I got the section together and briefed them on what we were to do. Whilst looking at the map I had made a plan with my other team commander as to the best point to set up an OP. We then mounted up and drove to where we would tactically set up position and soon got into routine, with a rota of who was on watch and what time.

We had been in situ for no more than a couple of hours, when a call came over the radio that we had been re-tasked to report to another team's position, to collect a pair of prisoners of war. It didn't take long to break position, mount-up and head to the location to which we had been tasked. We met with one of the sections from QCS who were carrying out a VCP when they stopped a vehicle containing two men, carrying sensitive information about troop movements and Iraqi intelligence. With my other team commander, I was briefed on the details and then we briefed the section on what we were going to do. The two men were separated, searched, tied up and blindfolded. We put one prisoner into the back of each Land Rover and drove to report to my Flight Commander at his position. Both men were taken out of the vehicles and guarded. They were still blindfolded, so they were not able to see where we were, or the route we took. After a brief report with my boss we were given the new location for Squadron Headquarters so that these men could be handed over and processed down the chain.

We mounted up and headed out to the Headquarters location. There I met with the Warrant Officer and handed the prisoners over to lads on HQ Flight who would take over the guarding of them. The lads on the section carried out this task as trained. The prisoners had a real look of terror on their faces; we were very firm with them but fair. We weren't there to be pals with them and have a brew or a chat. Once HQ had taken custody of them, I listened as the Warrant Officer explained to them through an interpreter that they would be placed inside a tent. If they stepped outside or tried to escape, they would be shot. They would be held until handed over to the appropriate authorities who would deal with them. By this time, it was getting near first light and we were tasked to liaise with Military Police at the border check point where they had secured the border crossing point for logistics to cross into Iraq.

After our task at the check point was finished, we reported to the Flight Sergeant and were briefed to make our way up to the top of the Jebel Sanam and liaise with my section corporal who had been attached to the sniper team on entering Iraq. My corporal then took over command of the section and I was re-tasked to be his driver. Our orders were now to dig-in and set up a constructed OP at the top of the Jebel.

On looking around, it was clear that whatever had originally been on top of the Jebel had been completely obliterated. The only visible remains were the warped and bent wreckage of a huge antenna. Any other buildings were completely taken out. The poor Iraqi soldiers that were stationed up here at the time of the attack did not have a chance and there were certainly no remains that they were up here. We spent a few hours digging-in, constructing the OP and also digging out a rest area to the rear. Word came over the radio that my section was to report to the checkpoint where friendly callsigns were crossing the border into Iraq.

Tonto, my Corporal, briefed us all and we mounted up and drove down the windy and very dangerous track that ran up and down the Jebel. Driving in these conditions certainly tested your driving skills and I was soon to be very much put to the test in the coming days and weeks. We reported to the checkpoint and we had more familiarity with our surroundings now. The checkpoint was just to the south of Safwan town, which was the main centre of local population in the area, with the Jebel Sanam and Safwan airstrip to the west. A road or track had been cleared for convoys to cross into Iraq and skirt around the edge of town; this was to be the main supply route for all convoys coming into Iraq and to push north as the war advanced.

A large group of locals were now gathering at the south end of the town, coming to see what was going on. Tonto briefed us that we were to park about a hundred yards north of the check point, and to deploy on foot just in front of the vehicles as security, to stop anyone getting closer. We were to remain until reinforcements arrived who would take over security of the border crossing. Something of a stand-off began between us and the crowd, who I would say were mainly young men of around late teenage to early twenties. We could feel the tension as they got closer and we were poised, ready for any potential trouble. Eye contact was really prevalent now as I eyed these young men and they eyed me and the lads, as if they were testing us, to see what we were made of. I could sense that there could be trouble any minute; any one of these guys could be Iraqi troops or sympathisers. I admit that inside I was scared that if they really went for it they would be capable of overpowering us, even though we were armed. However, I knew that if it was to kick-off, I would certainly take a few out. Part of me was itching for an opportunity to shoot one of them.

You could cut the atmosphere with a knife and the testosterone was high. We certainly tested their mettle when we were tasked to push them back, as they were getting too close. I took authority and with my hand on my weapon, started to shout at them to push back, using my other hand to signal them to move. We advanced towards them quite aggressively, shouting to move back, weapons in the shoulder ready to use them if we had to. They cautiously backed up. I could see in a few of them that they were sizing me up with direct eye contact. Without doubt, I believe that given an opportunity, a few of them would have seized the chance to take us on. I could see in some of them the hatred in their eyes and contempt towards us. But we stood our ground. After a period of time we were relieved by another unit and we made our way back up to the top of the Jebel and continued with our task of preparing and getting into routine manning of the OP.

I had been up for over 2 days before the first opportunity of any real sleep was to present itself. Our role on the top of the Jebel was to provide over-watch of Safwan airstrip and the friendly callsigns in the area.

The view was spectacular and you could see for miles; the airstrip itself, Safwan town in the distance and all the farmed area dotted over the landscape. As night fell and we got into routine and rotated on duty, we could see blasts going off in the distance, with tracer rounds being fired as the war advanced forward. Safwan airstrip was now operational and our Squadron were holding it and protecting it. Over the next few nights and days we settled into a regular routine as we continued with manning the OP. On a few occasions Tonto took his fire team, with me driving using nothing but night vision goggles, up and down the winding track of the Jebel to report to HQ. During one period we spent a full 24 hours absolutely drenched as it rained constantly. These conditions weren't the nicest, but then we were infantry, we were at war and we weren't sunning it on holiday at the Hilton.

I can't remember the exact number of days we were rotated on the Jebel, but relief came, and our section were to report to Squadron lines next to the airstrip. We settled into our new home and got a few hours' sleep. The new Squadron position was located next to the airstrip, with a high sand berm that had been excavated all the way around as protection. All the Squadron vehicles had been lined up in order, with accessibility to get in and out of their position by Land Rover when needed, leaving the trailer that stored all our extra kit in its position. A field kitchen tent had been set up where we were able to get a fresh meal, rather than the rations we had been on for so long. A water bowser had been set up with hanging makeshift showers, so at last we could get a proper wash. Our beds were military cot beds by the side of our Land Rovers. It was basic, it was still outside, but it was an improvement to living in a hole in the ground. It was home for the foreseeable future. We were tasked with various roles over the coming weeks, with daily and nightly vehicle patrols through what was known as our area or responsibility. Night patrols were something else, as we drove tactically - which meant no lights. I would be driving down desert tracks at over 70 mph using only night vision goggles, which was an experience and the lads in the vehicle certainly had to put their trust in me.

At times we were deployed to man checkpoints near Safwan town and we carried out vehicle and foot patrols through the town itself at all times of day and night. One particular incident that I remember occurred in the early days of the war. My section was tasked to help provide security for water distribution into Safwan town. It was very frustrating and became quite dangerous at one point, when the crowd nearly overran us in desperation to get water. The operation was very badly organised and controlled by a female logistics officer who had no clue. It was becoming chaos because of indecision of how and when to distribute this water. The lads and I were getting very frustrated and angry at the hullaballoo that this was becoming, because we were the ones having to try and hold the crowd back while the officer in charge finished her chimpanzee tea party and sorted out the distribution. At one point the crowd were right on top of us and I had to push an elderly lady right back and shout in her face to stand back. That didn't seem to deter her in her desperation for water, which resulted in me almost having to use the butt of my rifle at which, when she realised, she backed off. What else could I have done? As I think back, it upsets me that I had to do this; especially the thought of having to potentially hit an elderly lady.

Finally some order was restored and some water given out before it became a 'cluster' again. Thankfully, following this the operation was aborted. There were times when we watched on from our checkpoint as one aid agency or another would deliver aid to what had been a football pitch in front of us. We watched helplessly, as it was not our show or position to get involved, as the crowd would literally swarm the vehicles and ransack the aid packages. There was just no order to it.

The war moved through Iraq quickly and the Squadron were soon tasked to move to Basrah International Airport, on the outskirts of Basrah and take over operations protecting the airport. The army were tasked with Basrah city itself. When we moved to the airport the Squadron were housed in the bombed-out remains of the airport hotel; there was no electricity or running water but it was a roof over our head. It was certainly a welcome change from having roughed it in the desert for so long. Our area of responsibility would encroach onto the outskirts of the city dwellings. It wasn't long before the Squadron was in place and in full operational duties at the airport. The war moved very quickly and before long the war was over and we moved into the next phase of the operation, which was peace keeping duties, rebuilding the Iraqi infrastructure and training a new Iraqi army and police force.

It came as a surprise that, due to the amount of time 51 Squadron had already spent in the

Middle East over the previous 18 months, we were to be one of the first units to go home. Operations would be taken over by the 63 Squadron lads that would be left behind. In a matter of days, we had handed over operational responsibility, packed and were on our way to Kuwait. We were back in tent city at Ali Al Salem airbase where we were before the start of the war, having a few days to chill; we were finally on our way home. They even flew us straight to Lossiemouth, but there was no welcome home parade or anything like that; it was directly back to the Squadron lines, turn our kit around and head straight home. Frank drove back to Edinburgh and dropped me off at mine. I was finally home and just wanted to collapse into my own bed.

So here I was, home from war and trying to fit back into normality. I knew that deep down I wasn't truly the same. I had spent the last few months in Iraq on permanent high alert and now I was home, trying to destress and relax.

Kate seemed to act with me as if I had only been away on exercise. I don't think she truly knew or understood what it felt like for me to have been in Iraq. I had a lot of time to reflect and think on Iraq, on life, on everything. I struggled to relax and let go - to open up and talk with Kate what I was going through, emotionally and mentally. Now I had time on my hands to think about Sarah and the baby. Now the anger, the frustration and all kinds of emotions were trying to raise their ugly heads. I did only what I knew how - I bottled and suppressed them down deep. Emotions had given me nothing but trouble throughout my life. I did what I knew best, soldier on. I had my job and I had my old friend to numb and take away my cares. Alcohol!

Transitions back to normality over the coming months were to start to take a turn. It was as if a loose thread in my life was starting to snag and be pulled. Time on my hands was soon to be neither a good nor a positive thing. After having been to war, Squadron life became quite mundane in comparison and we were going through the usual routine of exercises, training and preparing for the Squadron to come up to fully manned strength. The Squadron went through radical change over the coming months after return from Iraq, going from a two Flight strength to the strength of a normal fully operational RAF Regiment Field Squadron. This consisted of a HQ and logistic element, two fighting Rifle Flights (A and B Flight), Support Weapons (C Flight), which was a specialised machine gun flight and finally Mortars (D flight). This took the manning level up to around 165 personnel. Everyone was offered the option to move to their Flight of preference and many new Gunners were posted in.

There was certainly a lot of change very quickly and the Squadron became extremely busy over the following year. After my post-ops leave too quickly came to an end I headed back to Lossiemouth to re-join the Squadron and to throw myself into my job. When offered the choice of which Flight I wanted to be on, I decided to remain on a Rifle Flight, especially as I had been made up to team commander again. For me this would be the best career choice, as promotion chances were on the horizon and I had in any case never wanted to be on Support Weapons or Mortars. With the manning re-shuffle I was moved to B Flight, 2 Section. I had a new Section Corporal posted in and a lot of new faces joined the Section, especially lads straight out of training. I became one of the 'old sweats' as the saying went.

B Flight had a new Sergeant posted in who had just come back from a 3-year exchange post with 45 Commando Royal Marines. He was a firm but very fair Sergeant. We also had a new Flight Commander, straight from training who was eager but had some 'interesting' ideas. The Sergeant soon had him on the right path, as the saying goes. I was back on the Squadron with a complete turn-around and I threw myself into my job, but the threads were to start to snag more and things were starting to unravel, and this is where I started to take the first few steps on the path to self-destruction and meltdown. I was again training hard in the week and drinking to excess, but heading home to be the supposed loving husband. But with each weekend that I was able to go home, when not on training or exercise, I began to resent doing so. I was withdrawing into myself and not opening myself up emotionally to Kate; pretending everything was ok. Things started to get strained between us. Kate wanted to start a family and as I didn't, I would avoid being intimate, making up all sorts of lame excuses from being too tired, to a headache, to not being in the mood, to even saying my sex drive was virtually non-existent. I was being selfish and was drifting further away from Kate as she was trying to draw closer. We started to just go through the motions of marriage, never really connecting as I was pushing her further away and drawing closer into myself.

Over the next few months, I was feeling
frustrated with life, with my job, with me, but
threw myself more and more into my work. I
volunteered for anything that would give me an
excuse to not have to go home at the
weekends, so that I could go out partying with
the girl I was having an affair with. I believed my
own lie - that no-one knew about my affair, but
for a select few. But in fact, the whole Squadron
probably knew, including Frank, my old
Corporal who lived opposite me in the block
and was engaged to my wife's best friend. The
pressure I must have him under, that he knew
but would not say anything, was certainly not
fair or right. I would even try and sneak back
into the block early in the morning before work
after spending the night with my mistress. I
would try and make it look like I had been in my
room all night, but everyone knew, even Frank!
My drinking was starting to affect my work.
After one night out I slept in on a Range Day
and had to be driven to the shooting ranges by
the duty driver. I nearly threw my career and

chance of promotion away that day. When we got back to camp I got a severe roasting and warning from my Sergeant. But somehow, I escaped with just that warning and kept my Team Commander position. But this still didn't stop me from drinking to excess; I just controlled it more. Or so I thought. I was in total denial that it had now total control of me, but somehow, I was managing it well at this time.

I carried on this reckless lifestyle right up to Christmas, still having an affair and then going home to be the so-called loving husband. My actions were really low; even when I was in Oban, celebrating New Year with Kate, Frank and his fiancée I had the audacity and cheek to phone my mistress to wish her a happy New Year, while my wife was sat right next to me, oblivious to the fact. Looking back now I don't know how much lower my behaviour to Kate could have been. After New Year I went back to camp and I knew that everything was to come to a head and was about to change. I was going to have to make a decision that would change the path I was on. It was January 2004 and I had initially tried to cool it and end the affair with Sue, but after a few days I realised that I didn't want it to end. During a night out in the junior ranks bar with Sue, her friend, also in the RAF and a feisty Glaswegian, pulled me aside and called me out once and for all, to stop messing her friend about, to decide who it was I wanted to be with and to sort my life out, as she wasn't going to stand by and let me mess Sue about anymore. I didn't sleep much that night as I reflected on everything that had been going on in my life, and I decided it was time to sort this out. I realised that I was living a lie with Kate. I had truly killed my marriage; it was at the point of no return and was time to end it once and for all.

In the morning I spoke to my Sergeant and explained briefly what was going on. He granted me short notice leave to go and sort my life out. I drove down to Edinburgh that day, stopping a few times on the way to reflect and work out what I was going to say and how I was going to say it. I suppressed all the emotions trying to surface and planned it like a military operation, with precision in how I was going to carry this out. This was the only way that I was going to be able to cope. I got home early on a Thursday evening and Kate was totally taken aback that I was home, but by the look on her face seemed delighted all the same. She was oblivious to what was about to unfold. I didn't say much and made up some lame excuse that I was home due to time off owed to me. Sat on the couch, Kate's sister was visiting; I felt out of my depth and was silent and headed upstairs as I couldn't handle what I was feeling.

After about ten minutes Kate came up. By the look on her face I could tell she knew something wasn't right, like we had been here before. I sat with my back to her as I couldn't even be man enough to face her. She kept asking what was wrong, eventually I broke the silence and without emotion told Kate it was over; I wanted a divorce. Still with my back to her, not even giving Kate the respect of even looking at her, I could hear the emotion in her voice as she started to ask me if there was someone else? What did she do wrong? Can we work this out? Again, my response was limited to no, it's just me. She kept asking if there was someone else? I kept saying no. There was awkward silence as I could hear Kate trying to hold it together. Then I heard her say tearfully that if there was nothing else to say then I had better go. At that I got up walked straight out of the room, down the stairs, out of the door, into the car and off I went. As I got up, I heard behind me Kate breakdown into complete sobbing. I had just totally broken her heart but I would not allow any emotion to register. Driving away my only thought was to go to my mate Andy's and arrange to go out and get wrecked.

After I explained to him that Kate and I had split up, he wasn't so keen on the idea of going out drinking, so I decided to just drive all the way back to Lossiemouth and to Sue. That weekend it felt like a weight had been lifted - that I was finally free. I did not have to be secretive anymore about Sue and now we could be seen as a couple - indeed we went out that Friday night as a couple. But in my selfishness and arrogance I had left a wake of devastation back in Edinburgh. I wasn't thinking of what happened but choosing not to think about the complete devastation of a broken hearted and completely distraught, estranged and devoted wife. Out of the blue I had completely destroyed everything she had believed in and known. Frank was now left in an even more awkward position, being grilled on the phone by his fiancée (Kate's best friend), trying to find out what on earth was going on. I can't, and never did, blame Frank for telling her everything. But as I said, I was not allowing the path of destruction that I had created to register; I suppressed all emotions as to me they were a weakness. It took Frank's fiancée to tell all to

Kate about Sue, about the affair, the lies and deceit. As at that time I was never truly man enough to take responsibility for my actions and tell Kate myself.

A week or so passed and then I was called into my boss's office for a chat. Kate had written a letter to the Station HQ and made a formal complaint that a serving female had been having an affair with her husband and had destroyed her marriage. Gone were the days when you would be given a 24 hour posting for situations like this. At least Kate did not live on-base and so there was no Married Quarter, and it was not an affair with another serviceman's wife. Not that any of these things made anything better. I had a talk with my Flight Commander, Mac, a good officer who I had served with on numerous occasions. Mac asked me what was going on and what the situation was. I explained everything to him; that my marriage was over and I was now seeing someone else; the Squadron Clerk from the RAF

Regiment Reserve Squadron on the base. Mac assured me that I would not be posted for this and, as I was a good soldier and this had never affected my work, no action was to be taken against me and that he had to follow the procedures in response to the complaint being made by Kate.

After that chat I started to get on with my life. The sad thing is that my case was not unique, but very common amongst the Regiment lads and the Regiment tended to look after their own over the hurt and cheated-on wives. Once the initial shock of the break-up had passed and sometime had lapsed, Kate phoned me and amicably we were able to meet to discuss the next step forward and proceeds to divorce. It felt so strange stepping into the house to talk with Kate after I had thrown the emotional hand grenade that had gone off in the house. We chatted briefly about how we were doing, just small talk, but soon we got down to the important matter of where do we went to from there. I had caused enough devastation and now just wanted to get on with my life and I was never materialistic. I reassured Kate she could keep the house and all the belongings. I would take half the debt and she would let me keep the car.

We agreed to a two-year separation after which we would be able to divorce automatically and cheaply. I agreed to pay half the lawyer fees. In my thinking I had done enough damage and wanted to make this as easy as possible. I also had my career; as far as I could see the Regiment would be my life until I retired and as I said, I held no value over 'stuff'. After all the formalities were sorted, we said goodbye to each other and even gave each other a hug. I remember looking back and seeing Kate watch as I drove away, and to this day that was the last time I saw her. Driving away, I could sense and see in her eyes the hurt and loss she was feeling and, driving up the road, I started to get a little emotional. Tears came to my eyes, a sense of loss was trying to surface, but I quashed it quickly and suppressed it down deep, really deep; emotions are a weakness, as I would keep telling myself. It was now the end of January and I had the rest of the year and the rest of my life ahead of me, to start afresh, to catch up on the so-called years I lost being married. A new chapter of my life, a new journey was about to begin, a journey that was not to go the way I planned or expected.

Chapter 6

So, my marriage was now over and Kate and I got on with re-building our lives. The damage was done; she was moving on I had to do so as well. My relationship with the girl I had been having an affair with went well for a few months, but then started to show cracks. I started to feel trapped in another relationship and felt she would start to be a bit controlling; asking where I was going sometimes, when I wanted to go out with the lads. I thought; 'hold on a minute - I had this in my marriage'. I was not about to start letting another woman control me and to be answerable to. To be honest, I didn't really love this girl; the relationship had been built on lust, forbidden sex and excitement.

One night, as I was alone in my room, I started to reflect on my life and on what I had done. I regretted leaving my wife and the hurt and pain I had put her through, but it was too late, the damage was done, and I had cheated on her so many times. I realised I had had a wife who loved me, a home and potentially a family, but yet it seemed that it wasn't what I wanted and I threw it all away. Regret was trying to rise in me, but I buried it deeply again. I had done what I did best – I had pushed Kate away. I was mean to her and I was emotionally and mentally abusive to her. I manipulated her by refusing to sleep with her, as she wanted children but I did not. I closed in on myself from her. I wouldn't let her near me and I pushed her away until it was too late. In my pain and anger I hurt her, to the point of breaking her emotionally, because I believed I was unlovable and unable to truly love. How I hated my emotions; I refused to trust or believe in them, as to me they were weak and did nothing but let me down. But in my emptiness, I looked to sex and alcohol for fulfilment, and a longing to be wanted, but I was always left feeling even more empty.

Like all the other relationships I been in, I had
not been faithful, even with the girl I was now
having an affair with. I pushed her away as well,
to prove I was unlovable as, for me, this was a
deep core belief. I had made that vow that I
would never allow anyone to get that close
again and I was certainly living up to that
promise. But I had my career, which was first
and foremost in my life; my identity. I would not
allow anyone or anything to alter that. In early
2004, my Squadron was busy with a month-long
deployment to Cyprus, for exercises and
training and and to conduct a final exercise that
would confirm our full operational capability. I
enjoyed my time in Cyprus, it was a great
experience. I knuckled down and focussed on
being the best Fire Team Commander I could
be. I was told on the grapevine that I was likely
to be picked up for my promotion course that
year. This was called Further Training 1 (FT1),
held at RAF Honington, the RAF Regiment depot
in Suffolk and was the Regiment's infantry-

based course to develop and qualify Gunners to be corporals.

During our time off in Cyprus we would go drinking on the ' Akrotiri Strip', a series of bars and restaurants next to RAF Akrotiri airbase. As per usual, I would drink to excess and oblivion. My problem was that after a few drinks, there was a switch in my head that would flip and that meant that I had to carry on until closing time or until I couldn't get another drink. One thing I prided myself on about being a Regiment Gunner was that I could drink! Not that that was ever anything to be proud of, but in the drinking culture of the military, the drinking was strong andfuly embraced. If you were a 'two-can-Dan' you certainly got slated for it. On our final exercise, consisting of a full Squadron attack on a village, I was out to impress, to prove myself as a team commander and leader and show my bosses I was a good infantier. My bosses certainly noticed, and I was making my mark on the Squadron as a valued Gunner. As a soldier, whether on exercise or operations, I was in my element. I was good at what I did, I could lead from the front and I had it all together.

But off duty I was a drunken bum. I kept myself to myself and felt the loneliness, but alcohol was my friend and I was would spend all my weekends off propping up a bar somewhere. Squadron life continued to be busy and I regularly found myself on military exercises all over the country; at times I felt as if I was always away from camp. But when I was back at RAF Lossiemouth I was spending all my time in the bars of Lossiemouth and Elgin. I was sleeping around whenever chance presented an opportunity or someone showed an interest in me. To me it was just sex, and I was trying to get my needs met. I went home to my parents on a couple of weekends when I could. On one weekend I got home on a Friday night, went on a drinking binge and ended up not getting home until the early hours of the Sunday. My parents were not impressed, as I had not contacted them to say where I was. My selfish behaviour was now starting to impact on my family, but I still didn't see that I had a problem at this stage.

I was called into the office by my Sergeant one day to say that I had been selected to go on the next promotion course in the August, along with two other lads from the Squadron. Finally, it looked like I was going places in my career; onwards and upwards. It was also arranged that the three of us, Jock, Boris and me, were soon to go to RAF Aldergrove in Northern Ireland to do a preparation course before attending our FT1 promotion course. I had very mixed emotions about this. This was my old Squadron, and the thought of going to Northern Ireland got me thinking about Sarah. Suddenly a whole range of feelings and emotions were trying to surface. But, being the hard soldier I thought I was, I buried all emotions and feelings deep down. I didn't need this distraction at this point. I had also started seeing a local girl from

Lossiemouth and had jumped straight into an intimate relationship with her. What also made us click was the fact she liked to drink just as much as I did, and we enjoyed drunken nights out together. But deep down everything was starting to try and find cracks and get out.

Nothing was really fulfilling me anymore. I even started to get a little disillusioned with the military and questioning if I really did enjoy soldiering anymore. I put this down to the stress I felt I was under, getting myself ready for my promotion course. The time came for me to head to Northern Ireland for my pre promotion course, and I was feeling excited yet apprehensive about heading back to Belfast. It was certainly to be an interesting time over there. I had mixed emotions as I stood on the deck on the ferry coming into Larne, so many memories of my time based in Northern Ireland were coming flooding back. Sarah was prominent in my mind, wondering where she was and what she was doing. The three of us drove off the ferry in one of our Squadron Land R and we were met and escorted by lads from 3 Squadron. It felt great to be back 'over the water' in Ulster, as we drove the route I knew only too well from Larne to Aldergrove.

That night we all went to the Bowl Bar on camp followed by the NAAFI disco, It felt as if I had never left, as I was drinking with my old mates from 3 Squadron. We had the weekend to chill before the course was due to start on Monday. However, as we started the course I became aware that I was finding it hard to concentrate and take in everything being taught. My mind and focus were elsewhere. I was finding it hard to keep my emotions in check and I was fighting an overwhelming despair that was constantly trying to come over me. My thoughts were also distracted toward Sarah. For the first time I realised that it was a struggle to not want or need a drink in the evenings. My sleep pattern had never been good at the best of times, but now I was struggling to sleep at night. I would lie awake for hours thinking about anything and everything. I was battling anxiety into the early hours.

I got through the course, but what should have been a breeze, I found tough. My mental alertness and concentration were struggling. We were to travel to Otterburn training area to carry out the practical elements of the course; putting into practice leading patrols and writing and giving orders for these patrols (all elements of what we would be doing on the FT1 course at RAF Honington). On the Friday before leaving, we all went out drinking on camp. I was flattered that one of the female stewardess had taken a shine to me and I ended up sleeping with her to feel wanted. Ironically, her name was also Sarah, and was very similar to Sarah from Belfast. With the drink talking, and lust in play, I used the situation to meet my selfish needs. She was in similar frame of mind; it was just lust, sex and a good time. Later that day, we headed for the ferry and to Otterburn training area, and with a heavy hangover I felt completely empty and unfulfilled. I was feeling down and lonely and even though I was in a relationship with Lou in Lossiemouth I had been unfaithful to her as I had to anyone I got involved with.

That second week came and went and I focussed, and got myself through the practical side of the course. I was more in my element out 'in the field' as it is known in the military. I was a soldier and these emotions that were trying to surface were a weakness and I had to squash them again. I was tough. I didn't do emotions as they were for the weak. This was my pattern of thought and I did what I could to suppress my emotions. Back at Lossiemouth I carried on as normal, doing all the final preparation needed to get myself ready for my promotion course. Things seemed to be going well between me and Lou, not that she knew what I had been up to when I was away. I convinced myself that this was more than just a bit of fun; that maybe I actually loved Lou and that this relationship could work out. I met Lou's parents and got on well with them. They seemed to love me and treated me as if I was family. I put Sarah to the back of my mind and threw myself into my relationship with Lou. For a while life seemed bliss. I was back on track and promotion would be only months away, after my course. Onwards and upwards. It was when the time came for me to head to Honington for my ten-week promotion course, that it happened! That's when it hit me! Everything came undone.

On the promotion course I found I couldn't function properly. I wasn't sleeping right, if at all; I was emotional for no reason and struggling to break the blackness that was coming upon me all the time. I found that I was craving to drink. I had no focus or concentration. I couldn't cope. I went to see my Sergeant on the course and explained I was having some difficulties and he sent me to the doctor at the Station Medical

Centre. I saw a female doctor who was brilliant; she was listening and seemed concerned. I explained some of my symptoms; lack of sleep, lack of concentration and low moods, then all of a sudden I completely broke down and burst into tears. I could neither control it nor stop it.

When I managed to regain some composure, the doctor looked at me with complete sympathy and compassion and told me I had clinical depression. This meant I was medically downgraded - I would be off my course and sent back to Lossiemouth. It also meant I would not be allowed to carry a rifle. This didn't hit me at first, but later when I acknowledged the reality of being downgraded and not allowed to handle a rifle, I felt gutted that part of my identity had been taken away. I was soon to experience the stigma that goes with mental health and depression in the military. I felt like a freak before the officer in charge of the course, as he explained that I was to return to Lossiemouth, but that I would get another opportunity to come back on the course at a later date. At least there was hope. I just needed to get mended in order to get back on with soldiering were my thoughts and reaction. So off I went on the eleven-hour drive back to Lossiemouth.

When I arrived back at the Squadron, I pretty much kept myself to myself. Rumours as to my reason for coming off my promotion course had arrived there before I had. Behind closed doors the stigma of depression had a few of them mocking me about being on a 'rubber-gun chit.' This was term used to mock those who meant to have lost the plot and deemed not safe to carry a rifle. The Squadron was also preparing for its deployment back to Iraq, and would be gone in a few days. I was assigned to the rear party. The few that were staying behind were due to be leaving the mob shortly or remaining because of injury. I felt gutted in a way, as the sqn deployed and left. I felt left behind and that I should be deploying with them. Suddenly, the

Squadron hanger felt like a ghost town, with only four or five of us and a Sergeant who was in charge. Now I was to report to the station medical centre to have a meeting with a doctor and discuss what was going on.

I was referred to the Community Mental Health Centre at RAF Kinloss, a few miles up the road, and assigned a female Community Psychiatric Nurse (CPN) to see on a regular basis. I made it clear that I did not want to go onto medication, as I had a real stigma about doing that and believed I just needed some time to get myself together. With the Squadron away, we would report for work in the mornings and be given general jobs to do, such as being duty driver and running errands; locking and opening up in the mornings - pretty mundane 9 to 5 stuff. I knew Ritchie, the Sergeant, well and had served with him when he was a Corporal. He was very good, in that he let me away whenever I needed to do fitness which was one of my strategies to get myself back to operational fitness. I threw myself into training; running and using weights, sometimes training up to three times a day. I got myself extremely fit. I believed that I just needed some time, and if I got myself to a physical peak, my mental state would come in line. I was seeing the CPN on a regular basis and she said I seemed to be looking well, and that my physical training was certainly showing. We would literally just chat and to be honest, I was getting frustrated by this as time went on. I just wanted to get out to Iraq to be on operations. Lou and I were now getting very serious, so much so that on one weekend I took her to Edinburgh to meet my parents.

I really fell in love with Lossiemouth now and could see myself settling in the area after my career. But I was also starting to become disillusioned with the Regiment. I wasn't truly content, as the job that had been my very identity was starting to develop cracks and I began to question if this was really all there was. I put this down to my not being on operations in Iraq, and the frustration of being left behind. I felt that they had gone without me. I kept my focus, but I got serious with Lou and I spent a lot of time with her and her parents, who I would call mum and dad. I had a real heart for them, and they loved and accepted me like a son. The cracks started showing though, when Sarah started coming to my mind, especially as every so often she would phone me out the blue. Usually, I just got a missed call with an answering machine message from her, but hearing her voice started really messing with my mind. Part of me yearned for her and I realised that I had never stopped loving her. Just hearing her West Belfast accent use to send tingles down me. I would sometimes listen to the answer machine message over and over again.

The drinking started to get excessive again, but when I went out I drank with Lou; she seemed to help keep a balance on it. I had also started working in the Junior Ranks bar as a volunteer barman, which was very enjoyable, especially as I was able to drink free pints behind the bar from the pints bought for me. I was sent to Honington for a few weeks as part of a team to train some RAF personnel who were deploying to Iraq on convoy duties, so at least I was able to put my skills to use, including being allowed to use a rifle to demonstrate how to carry out contact drills from vehicles in response to ambushes and attacks. We were accommodated at a training camp next to Stanford Training Area (STANTA) near Thetford. In the evenings I was allowed to use a Land Rover to drive to Honington to train in the gym. They were a good few weeks, and then it was back to Lossiemouth.

It was after a weekend drinking session, one night at a block party everything came undone again. I was completely out of it after shamefully throwing up in the block toilets, then heading back to my own block, Lou chasing after me. I had lost the plot. I had got it into my head that I had to go to Belfast to see Sarah once and for all and confront her. The problem was that she would phone out of the blue - I had no way of getting back in contact with her. It was always on her terms, if and when she would phone. So I had it in my head to get in the car and drive to Belfast. Lou was pleading with me in tears not to do this, but I wouldn't listen. I got in my car and drove. This was not the first or the last time that I drove under the influence, not that I am at all proud of this. But now I know that this was one of many occasions where the hand of God and His mercy was upon my life.

I left camp and only a few miles up the road, I lost control on a bend and put my car straight into a fence post, just off the road. I got out and looked at the damage. The driver's side windscreen was all shattered, the front driver's side wing was all broken and hanging off. I also had a punctured tyre. Surprisingly, looking around there were no police about. Trying to think, I jumped back into the car, managed to reverse back on to the road and in my drunken state, I decided to drive back to camp. How I managed to get back on to camp without being stopped I will never know to this day. I drove up to the gate as if everything was normal and showed my military identification. Amazingly, the airmen on guard duty opened the barrier and let me on. I parked the car up and went into my room to sleep where Lou was waiting and where she had certainly been sobbing her heart out. I thought nothing more of it.

That Sunday, we both went to the bar and carried on drinking. I left the car parked up next to the block, thinking I would get it dealt with on Monday. But first thing on Monday, to my surprise the RAF Police turned up at the Squadron to inquire about my car before I had worked out what I was going to do. The sheer insanity of it as I now look back. What must the RAF Police have been thinking when they saw the state of my car, and what must they been thinking of me? They interviewed me at the Squadron and I blagged some story about how I had swerved to miss a dog at the bend in the road and ended up hitting a post in the fence. Did they believe me? The likelihood: absolutely not. When they showed me the car was when I properly saw the extent of the damage. My driver's side wheel was just the rim. By the time I had driven back to camp the shredded tyre had come off and I was driving on the wheel.

As I said, I do not know how I managed to be able to get back on camp, let alone not be stopped by the police. I got a good rollicking from the RAF Police Sergeant when we were both stood looking at the car. Actually, looking at it I couldn't believe the damage. I then had to escort the sergeant and be driven in a Police Land Rover to show him the scene of the accident. We could see where the fence post had been hit but apart from that there were no real signs of any accident. The Sergeant said that the civilian Police were content that, as long as there were no casualties or serious damage to any property, they would leave it in the hands of the RAF Police. Driving back to camp I told the Sergeant I would get the insurance company to pick up the car and get it dealt with. He was happy with that and the matter was closed. I remember him looking directly at me and sternly asking me if I had I been drinking at the time. I calmly said 'no'. He continued looking at me for a few seconds then turned and said nothing. But I believe deep down he knew I was lying. As people would probably say, I was really lucky to have got away with that. I now know it wasn't luck in the slightest. It was the mercy of God and His hand upon me.

When I got back to camp, the first thing I did was to put the spare tyre on the car and get the insurance company on the case. They sent a local authorised garage to pick up and fix the car and I was even giving a courtesy car while it was being repaired. But even the shameful truth of this episode, which so could have turned out so differently, was not enough to wake me up and stop me from drink driving again!

I finally felt that I was ready to go out to Iraq. I felt that I had had enough time to get myself together - I was again the tough soldier I needed to be, out serving with my mates in Iraq. My CPN was on holiday, so I went to the doctor and convinced him I was ready to get upgraded back to full duties. I can't remember what I actually said to him, but it must have been enough because he agreed to sign me fit for full duties. I can't describe how great I felt, now that I could go back to soldiering. I informed the Squadron clerk and I was sent to the Ground Defence Training centre on camp to get my qualifications up to date in weapon handling and Nuclear, Biological and Chemical warfare. Once that was done, I got my kit packed together, ready to get my deployment details through. It was at this time, even though I was still married to Kate, that I got engaged to Lou. I felt that I was getting my life back together. I believed that I loved Lou and her parents were over the moon about us getting engaged. I felt accepted and loved by Lou's parents; that I belonged, and that Lou genuinely loved me. I believed I was happy. Even better, I was finally about to head out to Iraq and join my Squadron.

Chapter 7

I felt back on top as I was driven to Aberdeen airport to fly south, to connect with the flight out of RAF Brize Norton to Basrah. I was in desert uniform and was getting a few looks from people in the departure lounge of Aberdeen airport. I felt excitement and anticipation, knowing that I was on my way back to Iraq, any feelings of disillusion, despair or frustration were gone; I just wanted to get out there. The travelling was long and tiresome. We flew to an American air base in Saudi Arabia and transferred to a Hercules cargo plane to Basra International Airport. It couldn't go quickly enough for me, I just wanted to get there. On the final approach to Basrah, all the lights in the aircraft were turned off and the pilots flew in on night vision. All the runway lights were turned off as well, for tactical reasons, as part of the precautions against surface to air missile threat. The Hercules dropped into a steep drop from high altitude and just at the right moment it pulled out of the dive to land. It was pretty exciting, but the threat from missile attack was very high and very real. We landed in the early hours and I felt at home when the breeze of the Middle East air hit my face as I got off the Hercules. The wide range of different ranks and trades who flew out with me were all quickly processed and we were sent to our different locations on the base.

The excitement and anticipations of a warm welcome were shattered and not what I expected when I got to 51 Squadron's location. I was met by the Squadron Clerk, a female Corporal, who assigned me to the Squadron Snipers' tent, where I was to sleep. I saw my Sergeant at the HQ, but he was very curt, dismissive, barely acknowledging that I was there. He told me briefly that I would slot into B Flight where I was needed to relieve the other lads so they could get stand-down time. I wasn't even to be allocated to the same tent as them.

The Clerk told me to go and get my head down and report to HQ in a few hours. One of the snipers showed me the way to the tent and to which bunk was mine. So, this was home; a cot bed as we called it, in a mosquito pod. I unpacked what I needed and climbed into my sleeping bag. Before I dropped off, I looked about. The tent was very quiet and empty as most of the snipers were out on an op. I soon passed out and awoke a few hours later then reported to HQ for orders and to find what was to happen next.

The first day or so was routine; getting issued with my rifle, going to the make shift range in the desert and zeroing the sights. After I'd done what was needed, I reported to B Flight for tasking and to get started. Most of the B Flight lads I met up with seemed to be a bit standoff with me, and very distant. I sensed that there was a real atmosphere. It was as if they tolerated me, but were not as welcoming as they would have been in the past. I found this to be the case with a number of the guys I came across on the Squadron. I sensed that they were thinking "Oh; you finally decided to come out then". I truly felt like an outsider with the very B Flight guys I had been close to in the past, especially as previously I had been the Team Commander to some of them. I decided to keep my guard up and just do my job. I felt very alone amongst the very guys I thought had my back. Even my Sergeant seemed off with me.

But as I have said, I was a rough, tough soldier and I didn't do emotions. However, their behaviour and attitude towards me really cut me deeply adding to my sense of being an outsider. I was quickly into routine with the Flight's operations and I was tasked mainly to be a driver when on vehicle operations. When we stood down, I was by myself in the Snipers' tent and even when I went around to see the lads in their tent, it felt as if I was generally not welcome but was intruding. I then kept myself pretty much to myself and withdrew into myself. The only person who really gave me any time of day and treated me as he always had was my good friend, Kiwi, who was on the Sniper Section.

I found out from the Squadron clerk within days of being back in Iraq, that I had been picked to go back on the next promotion course that was to start the following year. This was my drive, my focus to keep me going. My thoughts were; be professional, soldier on, get on your promotion course, get your promotion and get posted. I knuckled down and gave it everything I had while I was on my tour in Iraq, doing just what I had to do and keeping myself to myself. This tour was to be quite challenging, as I will explain. I was on a routine vehicle patrol with a B Flight multiple (this is made up of a twelve-man team led by the Sergeant, split into three x four-man Fire Teams). I was driving the lead vehicle with my Sergeant in the front. We were patrolling south of the airport just on the outskirts of Basra city; up to our right on a bridge was a hasty checkpoint manned by masked men. We had no idea who they were and had no radio confirmation Iraqi police were operating in the area. As we were fast approaching but on alert, all of a sudden gunfire came flying over the top of us.

There was no mistaking the zipping sound rounds make when they are fired near or at you. It definitely sounded that it was coming at us. Suddenly training took over. I didn't panic, but automatically went into tactical driving and sped out of the danger zone in a controlled manner, while the Sergeant called out "Contact - Contact wait out" on the radio, notifying HQ that we had come under fire. All three vehicles drove a hundred yards up the road and stopped behind an embankment. We all dismounted onto the ridge and got 'eyes on' our assailants, weapons pointed, ready to return fire should the need arise. Corporal Jim assessed the situation, passing details to my Sergeant, who was in the vehicle relaying events on the radio to HQ. From coming under fire to being dismounted, with weapons pointed in a defensive fire position, took about a minute but it felt so much longer, as if time had slowed down. Everyone was in position, weapons at the aim and ready for a fight.

The Sergeant was calling in for backup and the Quick Reaction Force (QRF) were deployed and were en-route. We kept 'eyes on', calling out what we saw with Jim reporting back to the Sergeant what was happening. Ahead of us was a group of armed men in balaclavas.; they had pulled over a car in a vehicle check point on the bridge. All the car doors were open and there were two or three men lying face down on the ground, not moving. We did not know at this point whether they had been shot dead or not. The armed men were very edgy. All the lads' adrenaline was up, especially mine. I had a particular armed masked man in my sites, he was leaning over the men on the ground with his weapon pointed right at their heads. My weapon was aimed directly at his head, my finger on the trigger ready to fire at a moment's notice. At this distance I would drop him without doubt. I was so up for a fight, so wanted to shoot this guy; I had a voice in my head saying "do it = pull the trigger". For the first time in my life I so wanted to kill someone while also being in a position to do so. I was so pumped up and just itching for an opportunity to open fire. Everything in my career had come to this moment - an opportunity to finally get to kill someone in action. That was how I was feeling, I so wanted blood, to take a life.

We continued to watch and monitor as the QRF arrived - within minutes or so it felt. The Sergeant and a few of the ranks from the QRF cautiously approached the armed men, while we covered them in case a fire-fight was to break out. In the end, it turned out that these armed men were actually Iraqi police. They had pulled over some insurgents, but they had not informed friendly callsigns that they were operating in the area. I don't know about the rest of the lads, but as we stood down and returned to camp for debriefing, I personally felt frustrated and totally-let down that this had the potential of being a real fire-fight. But it did highlight the reality of the danger we faced every time we went out on patrol, and the uncertainty about what we might come up against. The threat was very high and very real. There were insurgents out there that wanted to kill us.

Only a few days later, the same B Flight multiple were on an early morning vehicle patrol. We were to the North of the airport and I was again driving the lead vehicle with the Sergeant next to me. We were patrolling along a tracked road when we came under fire. This time it was, without doubt, aimed at us. The shots went directly overhead of the vehicle I was driving. Even the guys in the back who were on top cover (standing in the vehicle hatches providing covering fire if necessary) let out a few cuss words as they ducked down from the incoming fire. Again, training took over and we got out of the danger zone and stopped the vehicles a few yards up the road. As the shots came in, the Sergeant again shouted over the radio "Contact - Contact wait out." We dismounted, got into tactical formation and, covering each other by Fire Team, we advanced to the point of contact, where the firing had come from. But when we got there, the enemy had run. It was a classic 'hit-and-run' tactic by insurgents. We stayed in our defensive position in case the attack was to draw us in to an ambush, the QRF arrived. After liaising with my Sergeant and getting the low-down on what had happened, the QRF carried out a clearance foot patrol to try and draw the insurgents, out while we gave cover. It was to no avail; they had well and truly run. We mounted back onto our vehicles and finished our patrol before heading back to base. All the while, I was feeling frustrated and angry. I was up for a fight and thought 'cowards! why don't you stay and fight, you stupid ragheads.'

Later, I found myself on another patrol, on top cover with another lad, providing cover for the vehicle multiple patrol. We were patrolling through a built-up settlement on the outskirts of Basra City and had passed a huge crowd watching a local game of football; they turned to see us drive past. Unfortunately, we had to come back past them and it was then that they grouped together to try and surround our patrol. The Sergeant had already anticipated what they were about to do and got the three vehicles to speed up and get past them. It didn't stop us from getting pelted with rocks and glass; both of us on top cover did our best to avoid getting hit. You could see the hatred in the eyes of the mob. I would hate to think what they would have done to us if they had managed to overrun the patrol and get a hold of each of us. I know for certain that if they had I would have taken as many of them with me as I could.

One of the luckiest incidents of the tour (as some would put it, but I would say it was the hand of the Lord upon us), B Flight were on a dawn patrol along a prominent dirt road, carrying out regular route clearance and checking for possible Improvised Explosive Device (IED) threats, when we stopped to carry out what we call 'five and twenty metre checks' within and around us. On checking a particular culvert, Harry, one of the Corporals, found something very suspicious = as if something had been freshly dug in across the road. On closer inspection and with carefully searching, Harry found it. Very well positioned, and hidden in the culvert under the road, was a huge IED. Harry liaised with the patrol Team Commanders and briefed them on what he found. Standard drills were then put into place for situations such as this. B Flight moved to safe distances and dismounted from our vehicles, getting into all round defence in case this was an attempt to draw us into an ambush. I was driving the middle vehicle at the time and my Team

Commander was Jim. We stayed in position and gave cover while the EOD boys arrived and dealt with and defused the IED. I wasn't thinking about the chances of what could have happened, but kept my focus on the job in hand. Later, when we were being debriefed, we were to hear the full report on this IED. The size of the device and the amount of explosives used would have completely wiped out the three vehicle patrol I was in if it had managed to detonate. It was also later reported by Intelligence that the device had failed to detonate and that it was almost certainly intended for our patrol, especially as we had been patrolling regularly in that area and on that particular road in the past few days. When I was on my cot later on that day, with a few hours rest before the next patrol, I had time to think and reflect. I started to question that maybe there is a God who is watching out for me. I also thought that I'm fortunate to still be alive; had that device had gone off as intended I would be DEAD. That certainly got me to sit up and think about life and what I was doing with mine.

The pressure and pace of operations on the Regiment lads was very high out here. The constant hours, regularly changing from role to role, with only a few hours off here and there and with very few stand down days, was taking its toll. But the lads were professional and got on with it. With the little rest time that we did get, it was hard to actually switch off and relax. Throughout the whole tour, like everyone else I struggled to truly relax and was always on a high state of readiness and alert pretty much most of the time. We were all constantly under a state of high stress. Every time we left the confines of the base to go out on patrol, we did not know what we would be facing or if any of us would not come back. I asked myself each time we kitted up and went out, 'is this the last time? Will I come back?'. Daily, when we were on patrol, one of the most frustrating things I found was to hear over the radio that soldiers had been killed not far from us, whether by fire-fight or blown up. We would also get this news on our daily briefings. It made me relieved that it wasn't me; frustrated that we couldn't help; angry that we couldn't get the insurgents for these deaths. On a daily basis when I had time to think, I would have a whole range of emotions trying to bide for my attention; anger, sadness, frustration, guilt, relief, thankfulness, abandonment and loneliness.

But, like the tough soldier I thought I was, each time these emotions tried to surface I would bury them deep. For I couldn't handle them, and I didn't want them. They were a weakness and needed to be quashed. One thing soldiers are gifted with, especially when under constant stress, is a sick/black sense of humour. I was no exception, and I was at the centre of a particular incident that occurred, about which I will explain. The whole of B Flight had deployed to what had been an old factory complex from which to carry out patrols. There was a rotation of Fire Teams going out on patrol, while the rest were stood down at the complex before going on our own patrol. We had all been given plenty of the classic packed meals, with cold pasties that you could beat someone to death with and it would still be intact. One thing in Iraq there was no shortage of was stray dogs and we had our fair share of them tagging along at the complex we occupied. One particular dog was brave and was hanging around. Out of boredom one of the lads threw this dog a whole pastie. This dog was literally skin and bone, and it wolfed it down in one go. Then another lad threw it another pastie. Again, the dog was on it, it even aggressively chasing off any other dog that thought it would get in on the feeding frenzy. That was it; we started feeding this dog pastie after pastie. We were in hysterics, struggling to keep ourselves together in fits of laughter as this bag of bones of a dog scoffed pastie after pastie. I was guilty of feeding this dog most of them. We were all betting how many it would eat before it had enough. With each pastie it ate, we were again in hysterics, watching it struggle but constantly eating them. This poor dog managed 11 pasties before it thought 'enough'.

Watching the dog walk off in what looked like pain, I couldn't help but laugh. That poor dog probably died because of all that it ate, especially as it was just skin and bone and its stomach would not have been able to handle all those pasties. I look back now and am very ashamed for the humiliation and cruelty I put on that dog, but back then my sick humour was something I used to deal with the stress we found ourselves under. Something else I would do on patrols, when we would liaise with families in the communities to win hearts and minds, was to tell the Iraqi kids I was an Israeli 'Jundhi' (Arabic for soldier). I would find it amusing when they looked shocked and a little scared; something I'm certainly not proud of today, and quite ashamed of.

I found that I had taken up smoking Cafe Creme cigars. Now, I had always enjoyed a good cigar, especially with a drink, but here I found myself smoking up to 20 a day. Yes, they were only small, but I had never smoked like this before, and I found them to be a source of soothing and calming. This became a comfort for me while on ops. We were winding down, near the end of our tour and going home looming in just a few weeks. It wouldn't be long before 34 Squadron were heading out to take over as the Resident Field Squadron from 51 Squadron. I found that I had a few more stand-down days from ops, and so headed to the internet cabin to go online. Through the Friends Reunited website Sarah and I had got in contact, and we were able to chat a few times, albeit by typing, but actual chat. It started to bring all the feelings that I had for her back to the surface again. Even though we only chatted a few times, it was clear she still loved me. She told me that she had kept all my old letters and photos in her locker at work. This contact was on her terms though. I was with Lou, and Sarah told me that she was still with the ex that she had got back together with when I ruined our relationship. I was then to find out that she was pregnant again with his child; another wee girl. At this, I decided I would not do anything to try and ruin her relationship, with my selfish wants and needs. I was initially happy for her and refrained from telling her over the internet that I still very much loved her.

Another incident occurred near the end of the tour that made me really think again about my life and the decisions and choices I was making. I was part of the QRF, on readiness to be called out at five minutes notice to move, should a situation arise. We were sat in the crew room when the call came to deploy. A truck that wasn't from the area was heading towards Basra City and had crossed over the dual bridge before the city limits. The driver didn't know that he had to switch over to the other side of the road when on the bridge, because part of the it had been blown away during the war. On his side of the road there was nothing but a huge drop into the Euphrates river. The vehicle went straight over and, turning upside down, hit what was left of the bridge support. There were two families in the truck. The two husbands - brothers I believe - had survived and were rescued, but badly injured. But when the vehicle went straight over, the wives and a few children fell out into the river and were swept away by the fast flowing current. Reports about the vehicle accident had arrived around five to ten minutes after it occurred. We deployed to the scene at the river side to desperately try and help in searching for the missing family members. But there was no lighting and it was completely dark when the truck went over. There was nothing we could do; they were dead and had been swept away. They never stood a chance. On patrol the next day, we drove over the bridge and saw the wreck of the vehicle upside down on the support. What carnage! It made me start to think about how fragile life was but honestly, I didn't much care, as I really didn't hold any value over my own life. My thought at that time was; when my time's up, it's up.

But on the whole I loved being a soldier, I loved serving on operations; this was who I was, this was my identity. Bruce, the tough RAF Regiment Gunner (so my thinking went at that time.) It wasn't long before 34 Squadron had arrived and finally taken over operations. Finally, we were stood down and had no more operational duties to carry out. Home was in sight - only a few days away - and we were actually allowed to have a drink in the bar on tha base. Officially we were only meant to have our allocated two cans of beer, but everyone ignored that and most of us got wrecked. I hadn't slept so deeply after that night of drinking since coming to Iraq on my second tour. The next day we were in the departure lounge at Basra International Airport, and would be getting a flight directly back to RAF Lossiemouth. As I sat there, exciting to be heading home, I thought about the future. I was heading home to my fiancée who I saw a future with, a promotion course, promotion then posting. For me I was onwards and upwards! Or so I thought....

It was early evening when we arrived back at RAF Lossiemouth. We were bussed straight to the Squadron hanger where our friends and family were waiting to meet us. Lou was waiting for me and it was great to see her. Some of us did not hang around for the superficial 'welcome home lads' and 'well-done' speeches, but went straight to the barrack block, changed and into the NAAFI bar with one intent; to enjoy a pint and to get drunk. I was at the bar with Lou, my friend Ryan and his fiancée ordering the first round, when I noticed a technician sat on a bar-stool beside me. I turned around to face him, to better hear what he was trying to say. He had obviously a few, and proceeded to mouth off about how he was back from Qatar, and what a great detachment he had enjoyed there. I was just turning around to take a sip of my first pint of the evening, when what he said next grabbed my attention. He started to mouth off about 51 Squadron and how the Regiment lads were a bunch of plastic soldiers and wannabes and didn't have a clue about being infantry (this was the polite version of what he said). By this point my fist was clenched and my back was up, I was about to knock him into the middle of next week. Lou saw all this unfold and before I had a chance to connect my knuckles with his jaw, Lou grabbed me by the arm and pulled me away. He was very lucky. Lou said to me "Bruce, it's not worth it."

I took her advice and calmed down. We ordered a taxi and headed to our local, the Clifton in Lossiemouth, and proceeded to enjoy the rest of the night – to enjoy being home and get absolutely wrecked. I was now on leave for five weeks, and what I thought would be a great time of unwinding and relaxation, began to fall apart. Now that I had time on my hands, the loose threads of my life that had snagged, were to start to be pulled and to unravel. What I thought was now to be 'onwards and upwards' were to be the path on the journey to self-destruction, that inevitably would lead to the internal grenade going off. I literally spent all of my time off with Lou, staying with her at her parents. The time was mostly spent drinking in the evenings and at weekends. One weekend we went to Edinburgh to see my folks. On a night out the emotions started to show. I was now becoming dependent on alcohol and controlling it by binge drinking, but at the time I didn't admit I had a problem.

One day, we had been drinking right through the night at Lou's parents and she had put on Elvis's 'Always on my mind'. Now, I have always been a big Elvis fan, but when I heard the Lyrics to that song, it really tugged at my emotions and suddenly Sarah came to mind and everything that had gone on, from the miscarriage to her being now pregnant again, came flooding back. It was as if the floodgates of emotions had opened, and I didn't know how to handle it. Then the stress I had been under in Iraq seemed to also release itself. I completely broke down and started to weep uncontrollably. I managed to get myself back into some sort of composure but my only way of coping was to get out of there. It was 08:30 in the morning, I was a mess. I walked to Lossiemouth forest and sat in a dip next to a tree in the snow-filled wood and for the first time in a long time I didn't fight what was going on, and I sobbed uncontrollably for what seemed a long time.

When I was able to recover some composure and started to sober up, I felt so out of control and helpless and this totally scared me. I started to hate who I was and the mess I was becoming, I started not to care about even wanting to live. Again, I suppressed what was surfacing and walked into Lossiemouth. I sat on a bench overlooking the harbour for a couple of hours, waiting for the Clifton to open. My mind and body were calling out to me, telling me I needed a drink. As soon as the bar was open, I went in and carried on drinking, eventually ending up at the Lossiemouth Inn. After drinking for nearly 24 hours, I called it a day and collapsed into bed. I slept for nearly eighteen hours, due to complete exhaustion. I was well and truly burning the candles at both ends.

It was time to go back to work and I found myself very busy over the next few months, away a lot, on training exercises all over the place. On return from one of the exercises, I was given another five-week period of leave, and I applied for permission to live off-camp and move in with Lou and her parents. After all, in their eyes we were engaged to be married, and I was loved by them as a son. I loved them dearly too. I got myself onto an even keel and focussed again. My promotion course was only weeks away. For a while, in the weeks leading up to my course, life seemed normal and content. Even Lou's step-dad's mum loved me, accepted me like a grandson and blessed me with her late husband's gold watch. It was amazing to feel loved and accepted by this family. But it wasn't long before I was again battling with the core belief that I was unable to love, and that I was un-loveable. I was soon packed, ready and on my way to RAF Honington for my Corporal promotion course, which was now sixteen weeks long, with considerable changes and additions to its content. On the course, every student was promoted to Acting Corporal. Once again, I put on Corporal stripes and only needed to complete the course to be fully promoted. I left Lossiemouth on the long drive to new horizons,

Onwards and Upwards? Time would tell! There were quite a few familiar faces when we all arrived for the initial briefing on the first day of the course, even a couple of guys from my Squadron. I felt confident that I was ready and would complete this course, but I wasn't aware that the pin on my internal grenade was about to be pulled and the grenade go off. The first few weeks of the course consisted mainly of theory and lectures, with various practical elements out on the training area. On the first weekend, we all went out together in groups to our old haunts in Bury St Edmunds and ended up at the infamous Brasiilias night club in the town. I got so completely wrecked that I vaguely remember one of the lads helping to put me in a taxi. To my surprise, with very little memory I woke up not on camp, but at a house in a local village, next to a girl I did not know. I took a taxi back to camp and got showered and changed, my only thought being to head straight back into Bury St Edmunds with the lads, and to carry on from where I left off, on another all-day drinking session.

I was struggling to keep myself together, emotions were trying to surface and alcohol was failing to suppress them. On the course, I was struggling to sleep at night and found myself staring at the course work, unable to put pen to paper and complete my assignments. I was struggling to hold myself together, with a darkness constantly smothering me. My thoughts were tormenting me and my emotions refused to stay silent anymore. I was restless. One evening I arranged to meet up with a South African girl, to try and escape for a few hours and forget about things. I had met her briefly in Brasillia night club on my first night out. She worked behind the bar and had given her number to my mate. We met up and got on well, but yet again, I wasn't thinking of Lou and how selfish I was being. I wanted needs to be met and to feel wanted, and she was providing that. Looking back now, I saw in my brokenness how selfish I truly was. There was a spark between us both that made me question what my relationship with Lou was truly about.

The week after I had met up with this girl was to see my downfall. We had been given what we call orders – a set of instructions from an officer about a mock operation. As Corporals, we had to extract the specific information from these to establish what the mission was to be for an 8 man team. We then had to write our own set of orders that we would give to our section, then carry them out. That night I was to write out those orders to give in a classroom the next day, under the observation of one of the Sergeant instructors. I just couldn't write anything. I couldn't function, I was sat numb, void of anything. Fearful, anxious, emotional, craving a drink but knowing that was out of the question, I was unable to sleep and my mind was in overdrive. The next day in front of the class, I thought I would try and cuff my way through my orders, but I froze - the pin was pulled, the internal grenade went off and everything, internally and emotionally, exploded. Out of nowhere I burst into complete sobbing tears. I can't blame him, but whether out of embarrassment or not knowing what to do, the Sergeant sent the lads out of the room, turned to me and just ripped into me. He bollocked me, shouting all sorts of obscenities at me, calling me all sorts of vile names and telling me what a waste of space I was. When he calmed down and I managed to get some composure, he sent me to the Course Commander's office.

It felt like deja vu; here I was again, in the same office, with the same Officer, facing the same problem. I can't blame him either, for being completely 'off' with me and frustrated again at sending me to the medical centre. The same doctor, still compassionate and caring, diagnosed me with clinical depression, signing me off and downgrading me from full duties. But there was a difference this time; I now realised that I was broken, but didn't know what to do to be fixed. I was at the point of giving up completely. I saw no future and just wanted the tormenting going on in my head to stop. I reported back to the Training Office and was signed off the course, to be sent back to the barracks to get my kit together. I was to be allowed to leave the next morning, to drive back to Lossiemouth.

I remember sitting in the back of the Land Rover, waiting to be driven back to the barracks and my old Flight Sergeant from 51 Squadron, now on the Training Wing, was to drive me back. I had a lot of respect for him and he was a great soldier. Merv was his name, and I felt that I had so let him down when he looked at me with disappointment, but also concern. We didn't talk much on the drive to the camp, just small talk. But as he dropped me off, I will never forget him looking at me directly in the eyes and saying to me with true, heartfelt compassion; " Take care of yourself Bruce." That really spoke to my heart.

I was all alone in the accommodation now, with time to kill. I did not want to face any of the lads when they got back that afternoon, especially the thousands of questions they would have. I reached out to the South African girl and called her. She invited me over and I found being wanted and accepted with her. We talked, and I explained the whole situation of my life to her and the journey I'd been on, even about Lou. She still wanted to stay in contact, and I did just that. I had contact with her on and off for a year or so, and especially for a while when I was back at Lossiemouth.

The next morning, I picked up my kit, handed my room back and proceeded on the long drive back to Lossiemouth. At this point I phoned Lou and explained what had happened, about coming off the course and being sent home. I felt even more of a wretch when she was so compassionate, loving, supportive and understanding, yet I was still operating in a web of deceit and lies. The drive back to Lossiemouth was a long eleven hours, with a lot of time to reflect. I caught my reflection looking back at me in my mirror. What I saw I hated; I hated who I had become, what I had done and what a wretch and a failure I was. I was a broken mess with no hope, no desire to be around and I started to think that the world would be a better place with Bruce McEwen gone. I was on a new path now - a path that would lead to complete self-destruction.

Chapter 8

When I arrived back at 51 Squadron, Flight
Sergeant Charlie met me in his office. He was
great; very sympathetic and supportive. I was
informed that I would be now on HQ Flight,
working in their building, out of the way of
everyone (which was to be a bit of a blessing).
The doctor was expecting me and I would be
seeing the same RAF Kinloss community
psychiatric nurse as before. I had a great chat
with the doctor, and I surrendered to his
recommendation to go onto a course of anti-
depressants. The chat with the community
nurse was very encouraging, and she seemed
really supportive. I just wanted to be fixed to
allow me to get back to normal and carry on
soldiering; It was all I knew; it was who I was. I
settled back into Squadron life, keeping away
from everyone as much as possible. I knew only
too well, the rumours about me that were
already going around the Squadron. I felt as if a
distance was being kept and I was being

shunned by those whose paths I had crossed since being back.

I started to drink heavily again. This was my crutch for coping but to be honest, even that wasn't fulfilling me anymore. I still trained, but again that was a struggle. My job held no enjoyment or satisfaction for me, and I now became disillusioned with the military. Even my relationship with Lou was strained, and tension was rising between us. I started pushing her away. I was believing the lie that I was unlovable. I didn't even know what love was or how to love, especially as I reflected on the way that I had treated anyone who was silly enough to get involved with me. I hurt them all, and pushed away everyone who had cared for me. I was not faithful to anyone. It didn't help matters now that apparently, I would call out Sarah's name in my sleep. But yet Lou put up with me and my emotional and angry outbursts. The more she tried to get close the more I would push her away.

I couldn't keep my emotions in check; outbursts would come at any time. There was a despair and hopelessness that would not shift. For the first time, I started to grieve for the daughter I had never known, getting angry at God and asking, "if there is a God, why?". At the same time I was angry at Sarah for having another child (not that I had any reason to be angry with her), while at the same time yearning for her, to hear her voice, to see her, to be with her. I knew I still loved her (or what I thought was love). I realised that I didn't truly love Lou the way I had thought, or the way she deserved to be loved and furthermore, I was still married, albeit separated waiting for divorce. I was in a right mess. I hardened my heart more and more, but I was so broken and hated everything about myself.

I started to have irrational thoughts and make irrational decisions, even though I thought I was thinking and behaving normally. I would go out drinking, intending to drink myself to oblivion in the hope I would not wake up. I lost any will to live and knew then that I was on a path to self-destruction, not caring who got hurt on the way. I was on the verge of a complete emotional and mental breakdown. I decided that my relationship with Lou was over. During the week, I took a room back on camp and on the Saturday, when everyone was out and Lou was working, I packed all my belongings into my car and left a note (a NOTE of all things!) that the engagement was off and the relationship was over. I moved back into the block and then straight into the NAAFI bar where I went on an all-day session. Lou was absolutely distraught when she got back and found the note; her stepdad had to console her. Not only was she devastated, but so were her parents, who had loved me like a son. When Lou tried to get a hold of me to get answers, I would only respond by text.

 The Squadron was away on exercise, so the HQ was very quiet, with only a few people around.

The following week was to be when I had the complete and utter breakdown. I was out drinking nearly every night that week. Each day, I was slipping more and more towards self-destruction. That weekend, I went on a complete drinking binge; I was completely at the end of myself and had totally given up. On the Sunday evening I sat in the Rock bar in Lossiemouth, reflecting on where my life had come to and the mess I was in. I thought of the destruction, hurt and pain I had caused to others. I looked in the mirror behind the bar and I hated who looked back at me.

That night, when I got back to my room, the pain and torment I was experiencing was too much. I lost the will to fight anymore and decided I was better off dead. That was when I took an overdose. I took all the anti-depressants I had, then passed out, unconscious. The following morning, one of my work colleagues came to my room, as I hadn't reported in for work. He found me slumped on the floor, in a semi unconscious state. I slurred some mumbled words to him, but can't remember what I said. The next thing I knew I had a female RAF medic with me, trying to keep me awake as I drifted in and out of consciousness. I vaguely remember being escorted into an ambulance and taken to A & E in Elgin. I was kept in all day as I slowly became compos mentis from the alcohol and the overdose.

They discharged me that afternoon and I was escorted back to camp and to the Squadron orderly room. There I was met by my old B Flight Sergeant, who was very compassionate and supportive. I spoke to my community nurse over the phone and, after a chat, she trusted me to be able to go back to my room and to meet with her the next day, on the proviso that I was not to go anywhere else and especially not to leave camp. I went back to my room and slept. The next day I met up with my community nurse and, after a chat about the previous twenty-four hours, she encouraged me to go to an establishment in Glasgow the following day, where I would receive special support and care (If I had refused I know I would have been ordered or forced to go). I put up no fight. I was completely broken, void of any emotional response or fight in me. That night I was again trusted to stay in my room, and late the following afternoon I was driven to Glasgow, escorted by the same female medic who had dealt with me the previous day. I drifted in and out of sleep all the way; I was completely physically and emotionally exhausted. One thing I do remember is that it was July 5th; the G8 summit was on and it was only two days before the London 7/7 terror attack took place. It was on July 4th 2004 that I had tried to take my own life.

That night, on arriving at the Priory hospital on the south side of Glasgow, I was met by two community nurses Paul (who was to prove very helpful to me during my stay and someone I trusted) and a female nurse called Barbara.

They helped me to my room and to settle in. I was initially placed in the observation room, where all newly admitted inpatients were put. I got into bed and completely passed out through exhaustion. I had never had the shakes as badly as they were just then, when I wasn't passed out through sheer emotional and physical exhaustion. The first couple of days in the Priory were quite a blur for me. Between bouts of sleep, I vaguely remember having chats with a few different doctors and nurses. But mainly I slept, and when I was awake, I was going through the worst 'cold turkey' I had ever experienced.

For probably most of the previous few months, I never had gone more than a day or two without alcohol in my system. Now my body was crying out for it as my system was finally detoxing. I was in the observation room until the weekend, but on the Friday, I ventured out of my room for the first time. I would mainly chat to Paul, as I built up a trust with him. At the weekend he accompanied me on my first walk to get fresh air. I would open up to him about my life; he was a great listener and support for me in the Priory. On that Friday, when I managed to finally enter the dining area for tea, I found there to be some other servicemen. Lads from the Marines, a sailor and a lad from the army. Naturally, all the military lads congregated together. There was a whole mix of people in the Priory with a whole range of issues. The military lads were in for similar reasons as me, with a similar story to tell. At least I had people to connect with. I wasn't allowed out on my own until the second weekend, but I must admit I felt safe in the Priory. I was assigned a female nurse from Arran who was my support nurse, and to whom I could go to with any issues. I felt that I could trust her. After the first weekend, I started on the various therapy sessions that ran during the week, ranging from group sessions, workshops, relaxation (which was far from relaxing - we had to listen to some annoying new-age nonsense and 'zone-out' meditation. I came out more wound up wanting to kick the nurse's head in for making sit through these sessions). We had cognitive therapy and one-to-one sessions with our support nurse.

I was actually able to let my guard down and felt that I was getting some help while a resident at the Priory. I had a good laugh with the military lads. In my second week, the Officer in charge of the Mental Health centre at RAF Kinloss paid me a visit. He was very much to the point and extremely abrupt. He said that if anything like this happened again, I was out of the military. It was the way he dealt with me, offering no support or compassion, that made me come out of that meeting agitated, annoyed at the way he had treated me and wanting to kick his head. Like I needed this right now. My support nurse was furious when I told her, after she had asked me what was wrong.

I was settled in the Priory. It gave me time to think and Sarah was seldom off my mind. They let me out to go and train at a local gym, which was a great release for me. I ended up getting a couple of tattoos when I was trusted to go out alone at the weekend for a few hours. I wanted to get a tattoo to remember my wee girl. From the chats I had with Sarah, 'Sarah' was going to be my daughter's name. I remember asking her what she would have called the baby if it had been a boy. I remember her saying, "I would have called him Bruce, after his daddy." It really touched my heart when she said that. So, I decided to get tattooed on my back 'SARAH I will never forget you.' This was my own special way to remember her. The following week I went to get another tattoo which has quite a story to tell. Even now, I believe that this tattoo was chosen by God Himself for me.

I was looking at the choices on the Tattoo parlour's wall and it was as if this tattoo stood out among all of them and was the one I was meant to have. The tattoo was of a cross with a banner wrapped around it saying, "Only God can judge me." For where I was in my life at that time, this was the tattoo for me, so I had it done on my right inner forearm, and it has such significance for me to this day.

It was about this time that I met Lisa in the Priory. She was an outpatient and only came in during the day, from Monday to Friday. We seemed to connect, and a friendship arose. I felt an attraction to her but wasn't sure if she felt the same. I made another good friend, Colin, who was also an outpatient. The three of us seemed to form a little unit, and would hang out together during breaks and lunch. The military guys had all been discharged at this point, bar one of them - a sailor. My time in the Priory seemed to sail by and as I said, it felt like a safe place and I could relax and let my guard down at. A month soon passed, and I was to be discharged at the weekend. On the Thursday, I plucked up the courage to ask Lisa if she wanted to go for a coffee that night, to which she said yes.

The night before I was to be discharged, we went for a coffee and there was a mutual attraction. But I also believed that we were attracted to each other; both being in the Priory and with our own needs. A friendship was truly established and on Friday I was discharged and sent back to Lossiemouth. I was given a rail warrant and taken to the station by a RAF Sergeant from the Glasgow careers office. I was texting Lisa whilst I was on the train. But when I got to Inverness I caved-in to the temptation that was knocking at my door, and went straight to the bar for a drink while waiting for my train to Elgin. After 3 or 4 pints everything was coming back; the craving to drink myself to oblivion, but it also felt as if the darkness was whispering in my ear again saying, "Hello Bruce, you didn't think you could get away from me did you?"

I arrived back at Lossiemouth, back to my room, where I had tried to take my own life. I was left to head back north on my own, and to report for work on the Monday morning. I took one look at my room dropped my bags and went straight to the bar. I got absolutely wrecked that night, and the despair came flooding back; the torment in my mind was raging. I ended up back in my room in floods of tears struggling to hold it together. That night I phoned Lisa and she told me to drive to Glasgow to see her the next day. That's what I did, and that weekend we entered into a full blown intimate relationship, which was not the best thing to do, especially as we both were patients of the Priory. It was as if we were able to meet each other's needs, but in time to come, this relationship would eventually also become quite volatile and unhealthy.

After that weekend I reported for work and a review with the doctor. She wanted to put me back to duties, but I said I just wasn't ready to return to work. I was given a few days sick leave and so decided to head straight back to Glasgow and spend that time with Lisa. On returning to work it wasn't long before I completely relapsed and lost the plot again. I became suicidal and struggled to control my craving for drinking. I was a total mess again and went through another complete breakdown. After a few suicide attempts, I ended up once more in the psychiatric ward in Elgin hospital. I had tried to cut my wrists, throw myself in front of a car and also drown myself in the sea, all the while getting completely wrecked to pluck up the courage to do so. I had cried out to Lisa on the 'phone in my desperation, and she in turn telephoned the RAF Police.

My life was completely out of control. When I was about to throw myself in front of a car, the civilian police stopped me. Having now ended up back in hospital, I was climbing up the wall. After a week, in a review by one of the doctors, I managed to somehow convince him to discharge me that day. After a weekend in Glasgow I went back to work, but completely relapsed that week. I was just so broken, and it was then that I tried to hang myself in the accommodation block, from the stairwell. Again, something intervened.

I failed to report for work one morning; I was completely out of it due to a severe drinking binge the night before. I was stood to attention before the Squadron Warrant Officer, being severely ripped into and shouted at, all the while totally embarrassed, totally broken, totally ashamed, reflecting how I had gone from being a good soldier, to becoming a complete wreck and an embarrassment. I was ordered to go and see the doctor and, on entering the medical centre, I completely broke down. I was completely out of control; I was a tormented soul. I was broken. That week I was ordered to RAF Kinloss, to the Psychiatric and Mental Health Centre to see Colonel Gamble, an army doctor who was doing what he could to try and get me posted and relocated to another station. Within minutes of my meeting with him, the RAF Officer I had met at the Priory came bursting in. He excused Colonel Gamble, sat down and looked me directly in the eye. He bluntly put it, "I've had enough of you. Your career is over. You're getting put forward for a medical discharge. Pack your bags, go home, you're on sick leave till further notice. It's over." At that he stormed out. I was stunned to say the least, alone in the room in complete silence, processing what had just happened. It was then I realised as it all sunk in; I was a soldier no more.

Totally numb, I drove back to camp and went through the motions, getting all the paperwork signed at the Squadron to go on sick leave, then I left quietly, back to my room to get the stuff I needed before I drove home. As I was getting out of my uniform I was reluctant to take it off, especially my beret, knowing this was the last time I would ever wear it, I looked down and saw my trusted webbing, that I had worn through my two years in northern Ireland, two tours in Kuwait and my two tours in Iraq. I picked it up and put it on one last time, knowing I would never go on operations or exercise ever again wearing it. I took it off, got out of uniform, got what I needed and got into the car. I decided to drive to Lisa's for a few days before heading to my parents in Edinburgh, to explain that my days as a Regiment Gunner were over. As I left RAF Lossiemouth and looked back at the 'welcome' sign to the camp in my rear view mirror, it really struck home that my days as a soldier were well and truly over.

As the days and weeks passed at home in Edinburgh, I would fluctuate between there and Glasgow. I had a lot of time on my hands and a lot of time to think. After being at home for a few weeks, I came across a real working man's gym in Longstone, Edinburgh. It was what you would call a 'spit and sawdust' type of gym, but a real bodybuilders' gym at that. The owner was Rab, an ex-bouncer but a straight-up gem of a guy who would go out of his way for anyone. In no time, this gym became a home-from-home for me; where I started to search for identity. Rab showed me how to properly train like a bodybuilder and the gains were quick and impressive. I got to know a whole load of guys from all different backgrounds, from the military to life as bouncers. They became a sort of new family for me. At this gym I found identity as a bodybuilder, throwing everything into it. Rab also introduced me to a couple of guys who had connections which opened the door for me to eventually become a bouncer.

So here I was, trying to come to terms with my days as a soldier coming to an end, but also finding a new identity to try and build my life upon. I was still battling the demons in my head and the craving to drink, but for a while I was in control. I took instantly to the dedication, discipline and commitment for bodybuilding. I was searching for a longing and an identity and I found this in bodybuilding; it completely consumed me and became first and foremost in my life. I believed the lie that if I looked physically strong, and have it 'together' on the outside, then the inside would follow. I spent as much time as I could at the gym, training and taking myself to new strengths and size. Everything I did revolved around bodybuilding, a very similar approach to how things had been as a soldier.

During the time waiting for my medical review, I had a complete relapse, giving in to heavy binge drinking, trying to suppress the torment still going on in my head. In the end I deciding to drive to Oban in the early hours, with no care for my parents or girlfriend who were trying to contact me to stop me. Again, I was in a broken state, fuelled by alcohol and mixed emotions. On the way there, driving on the A82 (which is a bad road at the best of times), I drove at great speed, with no seat belt on, not caring if I crashed and died, not even giving any thought for other road users. Somehow I got to Oban in one piece and after a few hours' sleep in the car, I went straight to my old Oban haunts and proceeded to carry on drinking. I was doing my best to numb the thoughts and emotions and the torment that were trying to rise up in me. I was ignoring any messages from my parents or my girlfriend. By evening, I had now got it into my head to Inverness, so with little sleep and fuelled by a massive drinking binge, I got in the car and started driving up the A82 to Inverness. A call from my dad brought me to my senses, as I listened to the message. I then pulled into Fort William and booked into a hotel to sleep it off. I had never felt so ashamed of myself as I drove home the next day realising the worry and turmoil I had put my parents through in the previous forty-eight hours, due to my selfishness and brokenness. Sadly, this incident wasn't enough to give me the wakeup call I needed.

November came, and I headed to RAF Henlow near London, to undergo the medical board review that would decide my inevitable fate. At the review with the doctor, I desperately tried to plead the case to let me stay in the Regiment with promises of changing, but it was no use. The review was very quick and to the point. The doctor came in, looked at my file with a quick glance, listened to my sob story then bluntly told me I was being discharged and got up and left. It was only a matter of time before my career was finally nailed shut and now officially over. I headed home that day and then onto the base at Lossiemouth to go through the admin formalities with the Clerk at Station Headquarters. As we went through all the paperwork, I was pleased to hear that I was entitled to a fully-financed Resettlement package, which meant the Air Force would pay for me to do a course, to retrain for a civilian job. I was also told that my official discharge date was not until 12th June 2006, so I had just over six months of pay from the military. After doing all the paperwork, I headed home to try and put order to my life. Through my mate Rab I got a job as a bouncer in Edinburgh for one of his connections. I had already been licenced by Edinburgh City Council after presenting a door steward course certificate and paying licence fee. I was starting on the doors at Walkabout pub in Edinburgh working with a good team, cash in hand.

I worked on this door job on-and-off for a couple of years. So now, apart from being a bodybuilder, I was now finding identity as a bouncer. The guys on the door that night seemed pleased, as they had been informed that the guy coming to work with them was a bodybuilder and a soldier, so it was expected I would be more than capable for the job. It wasn't long before I was able to prove myself and be a vital part of the team. But one of the problems of working as a bouncer was that I took my anger and frustration to work with me. I now tried to live up to be the tough bouncer who was ready for anything, trying to relive being a soldier through door security work. I really enjoyed the work, the attention and the respect you got for being a bouncer, but there were days we got aggro and disrespect from drunken yobs, looking for trouble.

It was then I felt in my element, an opportunity to spill the anger and frustration of no longer being a soldier onto others. I wouldn't take any messing and at times I was very heavy-handed with people. With all my military training and experience, especially from operations, I was always ready and prepared for any unexpected situation. To be honest, when bouncing I was pretty much always up for a fight but concentrated on being disciplined and professional. There were a few times when I lost my cool and I will share one particular incident. Walkabout Pub's policy was no headwear on in the pub, and even though I didn't agree with it, I had to enforce it. A young lad had been winding me up all night, putting his hat on at numerous times, with me politely telling him to take it off. The last straw came when I returned into the pub after a break and came face to face with this lad. He defiantly put his hat on right in front of me, with a look of contempt, arrogance and attitude. At this I lost the plot and grabbed him, using his head to open the doors, while Rab, the head bouncer stood aside as I launched right across the street. The lad got up and started mouthing off wanting a fight. In a rage, I went to take my tie off and to walk over and completely kick his head in. But Rab stopped me and told me to calm down and take five minutes. When I came back the lad was still there mouthing off, but I was calm now and very sarcastic to him. He kept saying he was going to come back and beat me up, at which I kept replying to him as he walked off tapping my watch saying, "I'm on tomorrow at 7 pm."

I was getting more serious about natural (drug-free) bodybuilding, getting involved with the British Natural Bodybuilding Federation and a developing a desire to get up on stage and compete one day. Because the military was no longer my life and identity, I searched for longing in many things and being a bodybuilder was one of them. I would hide behind the facade of being physically strong and having it together, but truly I missed life in the Regiment; I missed being a soldier, the life, the structure, the discipline. I missed everything about it. I felt my life and identity had been taken from me. Deep down I was angry and bitter, I was broken but mostly I felt lost. Trying to fit in, the transition to civilian life was a struggle.

What was to be my biggest struggle was my last visit to the Squadron, to get all my paperwork signed and hand-in all my kit. It was early January 2006, and my old Squadron were making all the last minute preparations to deploy back to Iraq the next day. My final interview with the Squadron Warrant Officer was hard. He wished me well and all the best for the future, but truly I wanted to be going with them. I was quite emotional when I finished handing in all my kit and had the last of the paperwork signed. I was pretty much ignored by everyone, as I tried to make pleasantries with some of the lads. It felt that I was forgotten but deep down, I couldn't blame them as they were all focussed on the tour to Iraq. As I got in the car and drove away for the last time, I felt truly abandoned - how much I so desperately wanted to be going to Iraq with them.

In the following months I completed my resettlement training in Glasgow, getting my articulated truck licence and a few other qualifications that the course suppliers threw in. I carried on working the doors and bodybuilding all the while, still battling depression, suicidal tendencies and trying to control my drinking binges. I was still seeing Lisa and splitting my time between Glasgow and Edinburgh. My discharge date was looming closer, my life was a rollercoaster and a mess and I was struggling to hold myself together. I had patient and caring parents and a girlfriend who put up with my antics and turbulent life. If it wasn't for them I would have been on the streets. I truly felt like the forgotten soldier that I was.

I managed to get myself signed to a driving agency and get some driving shifts to get my foot in the door in the industry. However, the decent jobs required experience, but no one was willing to give me experience to get these jobs. So, I started at the bottom, getting all the shifts that no one wanted through an agency, in order to get the experience to go for the job I wanted. I found myself driving all over Scotland, doing all kinds of deliveries. I found that I enjoyed driving trucks and being on the road, and there was good money to be made doing what I was doing, so the path of becoming a truck driver was laid for me.

It wasn't long before judgement day came. June 12th 2006 is a date I will never forget. It was officially my last day in the RAF Regiment. At midnight I would become a fully-fledged civilian. Working an all-day shift on the door at

Walkabout Pub, I reflected on my life that afternoon and the feelings of abandonment kept coming over me. The thought of being thrown out with the scrap - no longer needed or useful, kept flooding my mind. The words 'not wanted' bombarded me. My military career officially over, I had become the forgotten soldier. Now I was truly on my own, and the only one who now had my back was me.

Chapter 9

At the beginning of July, I had managed to secure a full-time job with a removal company in Paisley and had also moved in with Lisa, to try and make a go of it with a new life in Glasgow. On a regular basis, I was also seeing a community psychiatric nurse in Edinburgh, and had been for the previous few months, to try and help to get my life in order. To be honest, this was more frustrating than anything, as I felt as though I was banging my head against a brick wall. I felt as if I was repeating myself at every session and, although the nurse was genuinely trying to help me, I honestly felt that she had no clue about what I was going through, or been through, and that these 'touchy-feely' chats were both a waste of time and were winding me up more and more.

I really enjoyed being a removals driver; I enjoyed the physical side of the job and that each day we were somewhere different. I enjoyed the diversity, as no two days were the same. It was good money, but I also enjoyed helping people to move home I enjoyed going 'above and beyond' for people. This attitude was certainly rewarded by the tips we would get. My first day on the job was a bit of an eye-opener, seeing how people who had never served worked, and their work ethos. One of the guys I met on the first day gave the first impression of being a nugget. He had obviously heard I had been a soldier and the first words he asked me was "Have you killed anyone?" My eyes were certainly opened over the next few weeks, observing how some of these removal guys would smoke cannabis, or even drink on the job. I mean; I liked a drink, but never in my wildest dreams would I have considered drinking while working through the day. I came to learn that the removals game attracted a whole range of misfits, but one thing I realised, regardless of their enjoyments, most of them were real grafters. Removals certainly wasn't for the faint hearted.

I loved the fact that the gym that I trained at was two minutes around the corner from the company yard; every night after work I would be training in the gym. Even though I loved the job I was doing, I really wanted to live in Edinburgh. Things between me and Lisa could be quite volatile. At times in an argument, I would take myself away for the day to have time on my own. In the late summer of 2006 I had another breakdown that would change my current situation. Deep down, for me things were not going well with Lisa; I was feeling trapped and smothered. I felt as if she was trying to control me, and deep down I was struggling. I was due to go to Edinburgh for a routine appointment with the nurse and I felt at breaking point. I was still on the books for the Walkabout pub as a bouncer, and I attended a staff meeting there, after which we all went out for a drink. By the end of the night I couldn't hold myself together. I had been putting-off the craving, but after a few drinks the switch flipped in my head - to want to keep drinking till It was kick-out time. As the night went on, the realities of where I was at in life were weighing down on me. Then something in me broke as it had done many times before.

The next morning, I had my meeting with the nurse, and I was so broken I had given up on myself. I told the nurse that I was feeling suicidal and I just wanted to end it all. I can't really remember what she was saying but that she said that she would call me that night to see how I was. But coming out of that meeting I went straight to the shop and bought the strongest paracetamol the shop had and sat on a bench, feeling that I just wanted it to all end. I took all the paracetamol; about 2 boxes worth, around 48 tablets. Then I walked the five minutes to my parents' house and was chatting to my mum on the couch for a few minutes. I remember her telling me to go and get some sleep. Before heading up to bed I went into the kitchen and stole as many of my dad's prescription codeine tablets as I could, went upstairs and took them as well before passing out, asleep. The next thing I remember was my mum trying to wake me up in the early evening, with the nurse on the phone telling me I needed to get up. I remember slurring something about taking painkillers before passing out unconscious again. I don't remember much after that, only snippets of waking up a few minutes at a time as my parents got me to A & E and the nurse trying to keep me conscious. I didn't need my stomach pumped, but I was put in an observation ward overnight and discharged the next day. In my selfish and broken state, trying to end my life, I didn't think about what I put my parents through when I took that overdose. I believe it was by God's divine intervention that night that I survived.

The next day my boss was informed about what had happened and I was given a few days off. I decided that I would stay in Edinburgh. Lisa had been told about what happened and although we were not totally split up, our relationship was on hold until I was in a place where we could talk. My boss in Glasgow was great and got me a transfer to the Edinburgh branch of the removal company, although for a week I still travelled to Paisley each day, to provide cover while they found a new driver to replace me. I met up with Lisa and we talked and decided to try again. I would live and work in Edinburgh but travel through at weekends to see her. My suicide attempt was put behind me, I started working for the Edinburgh branch and really loved it. I loved being back and working in my home town. For me, Edinburgh had always been home. I started training, back at my old gym in Longstone and every so often I worked the doors at Walkabout. I was starting to enjoy life again and seemed to be pulling myself together.

Lisa and I went on holiday, to see my sister and her family in Indianapolis. I hired a car and we took a road trip down to Nashville, Tennessee and Memphis. At the end of the holiday we spent an amazing four days in New York which was a lifetime experience. Even after four days in New York the novelty had not worn off and I remember saying to myself "wow I'm in New York." We came back from there and the next few months, up until Christmas and New Year, went well. But on New Year's Eve I relapsed; things took a turn again and I went in on myself. I was with Lisa and I just went really quiet. The more she kept pushing me to ask what was wrong the more I withdrew and pushed her away. On New Year's day she was hounding me to go to her parents for a meal. I kept telling her to go without me as I was really in no state to want to go. It got so awkward and so heated; I wanted to try and keep the peace, but I was rude and silent the whole time, withdrawn from anyone who tried to talk to me. That night back at Lisa's place we had a complete blow out, to the point that I told Lisa where to get off and drove back to my parents. I was arrogant, hurtful and selfish; I ended the relationship with no care for Lisa's feelings.

I felt truly alone, that I had no one, no real friends who had my back. I believed it was just me, a loner, self-reliant, with no-one who I could trust. These thoughts went through my head as I decided to drive to Lossiemouth. I was searching for something, but I didn't know what it was. I was battling the hatred for myself and who and what I had become. I was battling that craving, that yearning for one more drink. I just wanted to blot out all the guilt and shame and pain I was carrying the only way I knew how when I broke down inside; to drink myself into oblivion. Drink, to numb the emotions and hurt that weres trying to destroy my sanity. I got to Lossiemouth, parked, and went straight into my old haunting grounds and got a pint down me. My intention was just to drink myself stupid, I had no idea or plan as to where I would be staying that night. To be totally honest, my only thought was to hope that I would be dead by the end of my crazy binge. This was my irrational thinking.

I met up with some old pals that afternoon who were still serving. They had come in for a drink as it was their last weekend of leave. It was like the old times and we went on a session together. That night, at the Beach Bar in Lossiemouth, I ran into an ex. I was so far gone with drink, but somehow ended up at her place, where I woke up the next morning. I decided to end it all and took an overdose that should have killed me. I was so ill that day and night, but my ex looked after me. I was too selfish to really care and on Monday morning I drove back to Edinburgh, having lied to my parents over the phone about where I had been that weekend. I went to my gym and had a coffee in the chill area, chatting to Rab and the regulars that I knew. Internally I was reflecting what a mess my life was in and how again, somehow, I was still here and had come out unscathed by the reckless choices I was making, whilst not really caring about the people I was hurting in the destructive path I was on. I was a mess and I needed to sort myself out. That week I managed to get a new driving job and start to try and put my life back on track.

Over the following months I got myself focussed, through my work, training, working on the doors and more importantly, I decided to get myself in shape for a bodybuilding competition. Somehow I managed to get myself together again; the question was for how long. I started seeing females casually, but selfishly only for sex. I was not interested in getting into another relationship. Because I was dieting for a bodybuilding competition and it had my complete focus, I was off alcohol for a period of time. I briefly got involved with a girl from the gym; for me it was just sex but she wanted more. Then she said she was pregnant. My thought was 'like I need this right now', but I took responsibility for my actions and supported her. At a visit to a family planning appointment, it turned out in fact, and to my utter relief, that she was not actually pregnant. I stayed well clear from her after that, selfishly thinking that she was a bit too clingy. It had been a lucky escape but this still didn't wake me up to the risks of sleeping around unprotected.

June arrived and I was just over a week away from my bodybuilding competition, and I had started a new job also with a great removal company in Edinburgh. I was about to go on holiday with my mum to the States; life was great and looking up. At this time, I had got in touch with Lisa again. We met up and she helped with my preparation the night before the competition.; for the time being at least we were back together, in a fashion. I was on a high, as I was finally about to get on stage and compete at the Scottish Championship, in a natural bodybuilding competition. I was in peak shape and felt on top of the world, plus I was heading on holiday the day after my competition. I was so focussed, but selfishly using Lisa to help my needs be met in preparing for this competition. The day of the competition was amazing - the buzz of being on stage and competing was euphoric. All the hard work, the blood, sweat and tears, had led to this day. I was in great condition and looked as if I had it all together on the outside. But deep down I was still a complete mess. The buzz of the competition was short lived; before too long it was all over and I was left feeling unfulfilled with life, now that the focus of the competition was over. After competing, I reflected deeply on whether I truly wanted to put myself through it all again for another competition. I didn't 'place' and the competition of bodybuilders was immense. I had entered this competition for me to finally achieve what I had set out to do.

I headed out the next day with my mum, to see my sister and her family in the States for a few weeks, which was a much needed respite. Even though Lisa and I were technically back together, I was playing a dangerous game of chatting to women on the internet, craving attention from women who liked what they saw. It was really just an appetite of lust and womanizing that can never be satisfied. Deep down I was wanted to be loved by someone, but I kept people at a distance. Sex was the way I used, to get needs and wants met but without the commitment of relationship. The 'forbidden fruit' as the saying goes, was enticing and exciting, but it came with consequences. I was not only lying and being deceitful to Lisa, but also to all these girls I was chatting with online. Most importantly, I was lying to and deceiving myself, that what I was doing was ok and honourable. The craving for drink was again knocking at my door. The rollercoaster of my mood swings and emotions were tormenting me again. The self-hatred and battle of thoughts that told me that I was unlovable and worthless, wouldn't let up.

After my holiday I ended the relationship again with Lisa, as I felt she was trying to control me again. I went out on a complete bender and failed to turn up for a weekend shift on the doors at Walkabout. The consequence of that were that I was not given any more shifts at Walkabout and was banned from the premises for at least 6 months. My actions cost me my doorman job. I threw myself into my removals company driving job, which occasionally took me to London, sometimes being stood down on paid rest there, which inevitably turned into drinking binges. Again, I was working hard, playing hard and training hard. It was not long before I was in another full-on relationship with an older woman from Edinburgh I had met online. She had kids and as a couple we would go out drinking every weekend. I was looking to this relationship for fulfilment and to be loved.

I was becoming disillusioned with my bodybuilding and the feeling of being small, and I battled with the thought of taking steroids, believing the lie that if I got bigger, I would be content and happy. A friend from the gym, who I also worked with, got me to try Decca. He injected it into my leg and I quickly noticed results from the steroids; my strength increased rapidly and was lifting more than I ever had before. I put on size quite noticeably, but yet I was still dissatisfied and unfulfilled. I was still struggling with who I was inside and now I had the inner turmoil of battling if I really wanted to go down this path. I realised that I did not want to pursue steroids, injecting myself or popping pills to try and get bigger and bigger. I was gutted with myself for giving in to the lie of steroids and I now knew I wouldn't be able to compete as a natural bodybuilder for the next seven years. The bodybuilding federation drug-tested and polygraph-tested its competitors. The last good trait I still believed I still possessed was integrity, or so I thought. I couldn't bring myself to want to compete against other natural competitors knowing I had deceitfully taken a banned substance; I fell away from the competitive side of bodybuilding but would never walk away from the training. For me it was one last part of an identity I was clinging to. If I didn't have that, then who was I anymore?

Through another friend at the gym, I managed to get door work again at another bar in Edinburgh. I was now working at the Jazz Bar, which was an easier bar to work at than Walkabout. It was also more money, but it was quite boring work. The only real trouble was when once in a blue moon, some snooty person with more money than sense, having had a little too much to drink had to be refused entry. Boredom was the biggest threat I had to fight at that venue. Around this time, after a few months with her, I ruined the relationship with the older woman I had been seeing - pushing her away. Sarah had started playing on mind again and the frustration was getting to me of her contacting me out of the blue, leaving a voicemail me but having no way of getting back in contact. I even tried writing to her, but got no response. Out of frustration and having been on a complete drinking bender, I made the stupid decision to go to Belfast and see her.

I got in the car in the early hours of a Saturday morning, after a big fall out with the older woman I was seeing and drove all the way from Edinburgh to Troon. I have only snippets of memory of driving, especially on the M8 through Glasgow, I woke up the next morning in Troon ferry car park, having no recollection of the journey. To this day, I will never know how I didn't crash and die, or worse kill someone in the process. All I can say is that someone or something was truly watching over and protecting me. But again, this was not enough to wake me up, or shake me out of the destructive path I was on. I came to my senses and drove back to Edinburgh keeping what I had done a secret.

So here I was now, single and starting to think about Lisa. I got in contact and she reluctantly agreed for me to come and see her, and we entered straight back into an intimate relationship. I told her before we met up, of the woman I had been seeing and I kept telling her how I pushed people away and deliberately hurt them emotionally and mentally, but it didn't put Lisa off and she wanted to get back together with me. We put the year behind us and started to be a couple again. That's when I decided that maybe we should get engaged and get married. I did the romantic thing; took her out for a meal and proposed and she said 'yes'. We went to Paris for New Year and for once it seemed that life was bliss, we had a great future ahead of us, we could put our past behind us and start afresh. Soon after New Year 2008, I made the decision to move in with Lisa in Ayrshire, get a job back at my old company in Paisley and try and make it work. We had the focus of planning for a big wedding at the end of 2008, which actually masked the issues that still existed. I had even made promises to Lisa's parents that I would never hurt their daughter again - that this was for life. But these were promises I was unable to keep. The destructive and deceptive path I was on had not gone away and it was only a matter of time before I fell back into old patterns of behaviour and started being emotionally and mentally abusive to Lisa again. I was truly a wretch inside and I hated who I was. They say hurt and broken people hurt people; I was certainly no exception.

For most of 2008, life seemed quite bliss and normal. I was working hard and training hard. Lisa and I were getting on, preparing for our wedding and enjoying time together. We had a few fall outs, as any couple do, but life seemed pretty normal. I got involved with the local rugby club and started playing rugby again - I hadn't played properly since my school days. We were involved with a circle of friends; a good crowd of guys and their partners and for once, life actually seemed normal again and not the chaos it had been. I was trying to control my drinking by being the one who drove when we went out as a couple. Deep down I resented the fact that I couldn't relax and enjoy myself without being able to have a drink, and that I was not drinking when everyone around me was. I would be quite uptight. I got around this by drinking secretly, when on driving jobs down south and away for a few days at a time. I would keep it from Lisa, and a binge session every so often kept the evidence of my drinking at bay.

I was genuinely trying to make the relationship work, but I had my secrets and things I did in the dark. One of them, which I thought was harmless, was chatting on the internet with women in online chat rooms. I flirted with them with the intention of it being just that and no thought of taking it further. For me it was harmless flirting and I loved the attention, the excitement, the thrill of the thought that I could take it further if I wanted but. Again, the temptation of forbidden fruit. The dark and dangerous side of this was that it was so addictive. I went on these chat rooms when Lisa would go on nights out and I would stay in, so I didn't have to battle with alcohol. This was dangerous behaviour, all secrets and lies. I thought I was in control, but it soon had control of me and temptation was soon knocking at my door. Temptation to want to actually meet up with one of these women as they lived nearby. I had to physically stop myself going on line and would delete all my chats and information, a whole web of deceit, lies and darkness. Lust is a very powerful thing and it has the power to consume people, make them do irrational things and destroy relationships. It was nearly consuming me. Consequences of my choices made my behaviour irrational. I would be distant from Lisa, secretive with my phone, defensive when asked things. I was acting out of character and Lisa was starting to notice and this made her suspicious. In turn, this would make me get angry and defensive with her. I started to become emotionally and mentally abusive toward her, trying to cover up my behaviour and actions. Deep down I started to resent Lisa again; in her own vulnerability and brokenness I felt that she was again trying to control me and my life. This life we were living was very destructive. I started to resent the coming wedding and to ultimately resent her. I put it down to pre-wedding nerves and that this was normal. I soldiered on. I changed removal companies at this point and just kept on as I had done before.

Christmas 2008 soon came and went. Now it was the big wedding that Lisa wanted but that I just went along with to keep her happy. There were certainly fall outs with each other over family and the usual wedding dramas, but the big day came. I was actually quite ill on my wedding day but soldiered on through it. A defining moment came when I was sat in the vestibule with my eldest nephew, who was the best man. I had grave doubts and was seriously reconsidering whether to actually go through with it or not. I put it down to nerves and reasoned I couldn't do this to her on our wedding day. I did believe I loved her, but I questioned if I loved her enough to give my whole life to her. In the end I went through with it. It seemed to be a good day, with a nice reception. We spent New Year in Comrie with friends, as a newly married couple, and then entered into married life in 2009. Sadly, this was to be a true wake-up call and the reality of our marriage was that all of our issues and problems were still there. They hadn't gone away; with the focus of the wedding we had put a band-aid over them and forgotten about them. But that band-aid was soon to be ripped off, and the wounds of our troubles and the issues we hadn't dealt with were to soon pour out. Reality set in and we were in trouble.

Within the first month of our marriage all our problems and issues started to surface and the cracks in our relationship were now showing. I would get frustrated, as Lisa would keep telling me that I was not able to give the emotional support that she needed. I was getting frustrated because I felt that I had done, and was doing, everything I could to be a loving husband to her. I would ask myself what more could I possibly do; I was working all hours I could get to support us financially. I was tidying the house and doing whatever errands I could, to be a support when she worked long hours. I would happily support her with going to see her family and spending time with them, no questions asked. But it felt like pulling teeth to get her to make any effort to see any of my family. I felt I was pulled between loyalty to my wife and my own family. I had my issues, and I know I could be selfish like any man, but I felt like banging my head against the wall. I felt as if Lisa was being controlling over my life again and I just didn't know what to say or do at times to make her feel loved and content. We were drifting.

I felt trapped and I started to resent Lisa, becoming bitter towards her. I felt that I had made a huge mistake in getting married again. But I also put this down to the normal feelings that newly married couples can have, and in my heart, I wanted to make this marriage work. It didn't help that Lisa would manipulate and control intimacy when she wanted and if she wanted it. I started to feel rejection when I wanted to be intimate. I felt she used it as a weapon at times. I can truly say that I was guilty of not trying to connect with her emotionally, before any natural intimacy. Selfishly, I wanted sex and resented her when she would not meet my needs. It didn't help that on a daily basis I was still battling my own sanity and rollercoaster of emotions, mood swings and depression whilst at the same time trying to control the craving for alcohol that still raged inside me.

With the constant rejection, I turned to something I had always done in my life; I turned to self-pleasure and masturbation. I would fantasize about other women and the scenarios and fantasies I had always had. I never had issues with pornography nor become addicted to it, but this dark side of secret behaviour could and would have dangerous consequences. Anyone who says that pornography and masturbation are harmless really have no idea of the consequences and the path they can take you down. Because I was turning to masturbation to seek relief and comfort, it affected my intimacy with Lisa. It affected things I wanted to do and that even when intimate with her I was thinking of someone else. I mention this to describe how serious pornography and masturbation can really affect and destroy marriages. Insanely, I even started to try and talk Lisa into bringing someone else into the intimacy. I was getting warped and unhealthy, with lustful desires. I would constantly try and talk her into this sort of arrangement, to the point where Lisa even considered doing this, out of her love for me and wanting to please me.

I look back now and am very ashamed to have allowed this warped thinking and desire to come into the marriage. Thankfully this fantasy never came to fruition, but I'm talking about it to highlight the dangers of these things. Turning to masturbation, I wanted more excitement and thrill and that's how I went back to the online chat rooms, to fulfil the excitement. Yes, it was very addictive and something I struggled to control. For me there was the excitement of knowing that there were women out there who wanted fun without strings and who flirted back with me. It was a case of *'I could if I wanted to, but I won't act on it'* that got the adrenaline flowing. What I considered to be harmless fun would soon really affect my moods and behaviour with Lisa. I was always very secretive, keeping my 'phone hidden and elusive to any questions Lisa would ask me. This behaviour furthered the distance that was developing between us. It was getting to the point when I would try and take every removals job available, to be away from home for a few days and able to carry on my secret 'on the road' lifestyle of binge drinking and flirting with women in bars. I would also lie to Lisa on the phone when away working, saying I was getting my head down in the truck when in fact I was getting ready to go to the pub with my work colleagues. The consequences of this behaviour meant that I was playing a very dangerous game; the mornings after these sessions saw me regularly over the limit when I got behind the wheel of a seventeen-tonne removals truck.

It is true that, when horrible words are spoken, no matter how many times you say sorry, you can't take back the seed that was sown. Both Lisa and I were guilty of speaking horrible words to each other - that the hurt took deep root, especially when what was said was thrown back in each other's faces. What was said affected us both. It riled me when Lynda described the flat that we lived in as hers and not mine. She did technically own it, and she reminded me of this fact many a time in heated arguments. As a consequence, I never truly felt it was my home and even resented living there at times. For Lisa, it was very painful when I was nasty and said to her "You're not Sarah!" This was something that would come back to haunt me again and again. Now, I realise the hurt Lisa must have felt in being compared to Sarah. She knew that she would never fully have my whole heart, as I thought about Sarah and part of my heart belonged to her. I believe that Lisa felt she was second best to her. Words can have huge consequences when spoken in anger or in the heat of the moment.

I would say that my relationship had always been very volatile with Lisa. In her brokenness, deep down I believe she truly loved me, but she had issues I could never meet. I, on the other hand in my own brokenness, believed that I loved Lisa, but in reality, part of my heart still did belong to Sarah. I was also a mess; inside me was a very angry and hurting person. I hated who I was, what I had become and what I had done. I couldn't control my emotions or moods and I was in complete denial about my alcohol addiction. Daily, I battled to keep myself together and keep my inner demons at bay. I struggled to keep my depression in check. I was out of balance and out of control. I was on a complete path of self-destruction. In the May I had another complete breakdown and planned how I would take my own life. I decided to do it by carbon monoxide poisoning.

I planned it thoroughly. I bought a garden hose, and cut it to the right size, so that it would fit perfectly from the car exhaust to the driver's window, where I would hold it at my chest. Then, one night, I drove and parked in a secluded spot and set up the hose. I kept the engine running, with the hose to my chest, pointing up to my face to breath in the fumes directly. I had decided that enough was enough and I wanted to die. My only thought was that I wanted to be in heaven with my little girl. It was better for everyone if I was gone and couldn't hurt anyone anymore. My plan didn't work. I had been in the car for a few hours and I was still awake. Something I can't explain seemed to be speaking to my heart, that was not letting me go. I now know that if I had succeeded in killing myself that night, I wouldn't be where I hoped I would be. I didn't dare tell anyone what I had done and tried to carry on. I was existing not living. I thought that by moving to another removal company and working for a guy who poached me to come work for him would help. I thought the grass would be greener on the other side. But it wasn't long before this guy showed his true colours, and I would end up losing my job. On the lead-up to that, I was to completely lose it.

On the regular jobs south, I was binge drinking to try and numb my inner turmoil. I was breaking down and sobbing my heart out. I was out of control. It finally came to a head on a removals job to Newcastle. I went out and got completely wrecked and I texted Lisa in the early hours, telling her that I hated her and wanted a divorce. I was completely nasty, lashing out at my wife. On returning from that Job I ended up losing my job and I just completely broke down. I gave up on life and ended up sitting on the couch for days on end, not washing or changing my clothes. I wasn't even talking to Lisa, I completely withdrew in on myself, there was nothing left in me that wanted to even fight anymore. My only thoughts were of getting up and walking out of the door. I knew that if I had walked out, that truly would have been the end; I would disappear, and I would be dead - I even planned on throwing myself into the Clyde. At this crossroad in my life something was to happen to me that I would never have thought possible, nor could imagine.

Chapter 10

One Sunday, around the end of September, Lisa said to me "I want to take you somewhere - will you trust me and come with me?" I was at the end of myself and there was no fight in me to even want to resist. Recently, I had been trying to get help from a charity called Combat Stress who specialise in supporting veterans with PTSD, depression and mental health issues. I felt that I wasn't getting anywhere and the support they were trying to give was not helping me. Initially I thought that Lisa was taking me to Hollybush House in Ayr, which is a centre run by Combat Stress as we were on the A78 to Ayr, but I was surprised when she turned off and pulled up in an industrial estate in Irvine. I was very surprised to see one of the industrial units with a sign above it saying, 'Bridge Church'. I then clicked that Lisa was taking me to a church. I found it really surprising and strange that a church was in an industrial estate; my only experiences of churches were of old traditional stone buildings and ministers who had the power to put you to sleep with their monotone voices. But this was completely unexpected. I certainly wasn't looking or searching for religion or God, yet I was open to see what this was all about.

From the very first moment we stepped into this church everyone was warm and friendly, but my guard was up. Lisa and I sat down quietly to wait for a couple called Roy and his wife Ros to arrive, as they were running a little late. Sat there in my own thoughts, something came over me that I had never experienced before. I became extremely emotional for no reason and couldn't explain what was going on with me. I started to become so tearful, but yet couldn't explain why I was on the verge of breaking down emotionally. This was nothing like the previous occasions when I had been on the verge of breaking down, this was a totally new experience. Lisa looked at me, concerned; she asked me what was wrong as I was fighting back the tears. I remember telling her I didn't know. But what I was experiencing was so new to me, and I can only describe it as tears of joy, like I had never felt before. I felt wrapped up in a love and acceptance that I had never known or felt before. It was as if for the first time in my life, I felt a belonging that was so new to me, but at the same time beyond anything I could describe. I was truly broken inside. Later, I was to come to know what I was experiencing.

The church filled up pretty quickly and the band got up and started playing on guitars, drums backing singers and such like; it felt more like a rock concert than a church service. I was waiting for the organ to crank up but there was none in sight. The music was really passionate, and people were closing their eyes, raising their hands, some swaying to the music. I was just taking it all in but one thing I noticed was the passion in everyone as if it was truly heart felt and they truly believed in the words they were singing. At this Roy and Ros arrived and grabbed seats next to both of us, as the music continued into the next song even Roy closed his eyes raised his hands and started singing without a care in the world - I was blown away by this. Roy is a big guy and all muscle, a man's man, yet he was able to lose himself freely in worship to God. "Wow" I thought, taken aback by it. Under my breath, I was telling myself that there was no way you would get me raising my hands and openly singing like these people, especially when some were shouting "hallelujah!" - no way on earth was I doing that.

After the music and singing, Pastor Bernie got up to preach. He preached like no preacher I had ever heard before, and he had my full attention. He told us why Jesus had come to Earth, why He went to the Cross and paid for all our sins and how He offers us forgiveness, acceptance and eternal life. Pastor Bernie preached of God's love for us all and how He is relentless in pursuing each of us. In all my times at church, this was a message unlike any I had heard or experienced before. When Pastor Bernie had finished, he gave an alter call to anyone who wanted to come forward and receive Jesus's invitation of forgiveness and salvation. As we were all standing and Pastor Bernie was praying, something inside me started to stir. It was as if my heart was encouraging me to go forward, but I wasn't ready to - I was fearful. I froze inside with what my heart was yearning for me to do but I wasn't ready! After the service, while having a coffee and chatting to people, some asked me where I was with God. I replied politely that I had a belief of God in my own way and they totally respected my answer, without further question. I was still taking in what I had just experienced during the service when Roy came up to me and invited us for lunch. They lived not far from us and were on route home, so we kindly took up the invitation and went with them to lunch.

It was a nice afternoon at their house, chatting and getting to know them both. I was struck that Roy and Ros shared the fact that they loved God more than they loved each other. I couldn't get my head around this and I remember looking at Lisa and whispering, "How can they love God more than they love each other?" Lisa had no answer to that and looked even more puzzled by it than I did. We had a nice lunch and spent the afternoon chatting about life, family, our pasts and so on. Roy was sharing stories about his own troubled past, living and coming from the Highlands, a real man's man, tough, strong and rugged, but with quite a troubled and wayward times. He went on to share how God had got hold of him and shaken him from the inside out, and the journey it took him on to where he was now; married, a father, business owner and a committed man of God. Yet while he was sharing all this, I remember looking at him and experiencing a peace he had about him that I had never truly experienced. I remember looking at Roy and telling myself that I wanted whatever it was he had.

Roy invited us to come to a house group at their house that Wednesday and invited me to come to a men's evening held at the church once a month. Before Lisa and I left, Ros gave me one of her old bibles to borrow, and for the first time in my life I was truly keen to read it. That night I went home and opened that bible and started to read it. I didn't know where to begin, so I did what most people do and started at the beginning; Genesis. The following couple of weeks we both went to their house group. I went to the men's evening and we went again to the church; something was really drawing me in and I couldn't get enough of it. After a couple of weeks going to these gatherings, something happened to change me forever. It was as if a light had come on and my eyes were suddenly opened.

It was October 4th, 2009 and Pastor Bernie was sharing another powerful message. I felt as if Jesus was talking directly to me; as if I was the only person in the room. It felt as if He was calling me by name to come to Him and receive His acceptance, His forgiveness and his love for me. The message about the Cross, and why Jesus came and did what He did, made sense. I got it - I really got it - I now understood it all and knew what this Gospel message was truly all about; His love for me, that He wanted me to be with Him forever. When Pastor Bernie gave another alter-call for anyone to come forward to receive what Jesus offered, I knew Jesus was calling me and I wanted what He was offering me. I went forward and gave my life to Jesus and suddenly, it was as if the blinkers had been removed, and for the first time in my life I could really see. As I looked back into the crowd, I saw that Lisa had not come forward as I had secretly hoped, but I also knew that this was a decision I had to make alone, and a journey I would have to walk myself. My heart wanted her to make the same choice, but she had to make that decision for herself. For me though, for the first time in my life I felt alive. I couldn't describe the joy I was feeling inside, but I knew it was real, all so real, and having now given my life to Jesus I just knew that there was no going back, and my life would never be the same again.

As the days progressed, my desire and focus had been shifted to Jesus; I had a love for Him I never knew anyone could have. The things of the world that I looked to and that had my attention, had suddenly lost any power over me. One of these was body building. I still had the same desire to train and keep in shape, but the competitive nature of the sport, and all my identity in it, had gone. I had no desire in giving it all of me anymore; I saw that it was all about becoming an idol for myself. My eyes were opened to what was truly important in life and what was of eternal value. My behaviour and language suddenly changed, I no longer had the desire to swear or act in a certain way. Jesus had truly changed me from the inside out and my desire was to please Him and to know Him more and more. Each day my love and passion for Him grew. I truly couldn't get enough of

Jesus and of reading the Word. I wanted to tell anyone and everyone about Jesus and what He had done in my life. I was so passionate, but this also started to concern Lisa. She started to get a little awkward with me as the days went on. But I continued to want more and more of Jesus, soaking up everything that was being taught and preached.

My work colleagues and even my family were a bit taken aback by this new-found faith. My parents thought that I was going through a new fad and it wouldn't be long before I moved onto the next thing. But I can only tell you that I had a true encounter with Jesus and would go on to have more experiences and encounters with Him as time went on. Tension started to arise at home between Lisa and I; she was starting to feel that I had joined some cult and she was backing off from the church and trying to get me to stop going. In her own troubled state, she was believing in God, and voiced to me that she felt He had stolen her husband. She kept telling me to stop this nonsense, that she didn't like this new me and wanted her old husband back. I struggled with this; I couldn't get my head around the fact that she would rather have the old me; mentally and emotionally abusive, a drunk who could get nasty with alcohol, a liar and a cheat, rather than who I was becoming; someone who would love Her with the love of Jesus and be committed and faithful to her but that I could never be or do without Jesus.

The fact of the matter was that the old me was gone; I was no longer that person but finally realising that I was the person God called me to be. I was new in the Lord; very zealous and passionate for Him, yet very naive in many areas. I neglected Lisa in many areas of our marriage, but to me I was on a journey to become the husband to Lisa that God was calling me to be. I would certainly make many mistakes on the journey, but it was important to keep getting back up and moving forward. One thing I found, in my early days walking with

Jesus and as He guided me by His Holy Spirit, was that all the emotions, sensitivity and gentleness He had given me were strengths, not weaknesses. I had got it the wrong way around - I had suppressed them but now I embraced them. He had given me a new freedom to wear my heart on my sleeve to be able to talk openly about anything, and I now had a heightened awareness of my emotions and sensitivity but, yet a boldness and strength to allow myself to be vulnerable before people. A year earlier, I would never have seen myself being who I was now, and I would have cringed at the thought of being able to be open to anyone.

This is just a glimpse of the transformation and work that Jesus was doing in my life. I will share with you what God revealed to me; when I first entered the church and became so emotional, unable to explain what was happening with me, it was God was saying "Son I've got you and I'm not going to let you go or drop you." What I was experiencing was a manifestation of God's unconditional love for me. What God also revealed to me was I was like a wild mustang, and He allowed me to experience the things I had been through so that when I was to finally meet God, it would be His love that broke me completely. That's exactly what it did; the tough hard man that I tried to be was broken by the Love of God when He stepped into my life, when I wasn't even searching for Him. I had started a course with the church called 'New Focus' which explained what Christianity was all about, what God, Jesus and a relationship with Him was all about, what the church was all about and what they believed. Lisa came with me to the first session and that clinched it for her that it was a cult and didn't want anything to do with it. She started putting pressure on me to stop going to the church and after a while, to try and bring peace, I agreed to stop going, in the hope that she would eventually come around.

However, I did stick my heels in on finishing the New Focus course, and I kept my word on that. In a way, I went underground with my faith, in the hope Lisa would be won over and come to the faith in time. The New Focus course consisted of a series of seven weekly sessions and the last one was on the 16th December 2009, a significant day that I will never forget. That particular night, Pastor Bernie was at the session, and he shared how God had freed him from being an alcoholic and that he had been sober for nearly thirty years. I remember looking at Pastor Bernie then looking up to God and saying, "Lord I want that; I want to be free of alcohol I want to be freed from being an alcoholic." That very second God answered my prayer and I was healed of alcoholism and of being an alcoholic. I have been free and sober ever since. If anything, I now have a personal hatred of alcohol and can't even stand the smell of it. I have had so many people congratulating me as if it was by my own power I gave up, but I always tell them that it was Jesus that healed me, and it was only in His strength that I walked in victory.

That night, excited by what Jesus had just done and the miracle that had taken place, I told Lisa and also that I would never drink again. Her response disappointed me; she said, "Great! so we won't enjoy a bottle of wine again with each other." My first thought was, "when have we ever sat and shared a bottle of wine together"? I struggled to get my head around her not being excited that I wouldn't drink again, as it had only ever brought pain, anger and abuse into our marriage. It was drawing closer to Christmas and as I was not going to church to spend time with my brothers and sisters in the Lord, I felt my my faith getting weaker. I knew I would never turn my back on Jesus, but I was really struggling. Things at home still weren't great, in fact the tension was still rising between us and my hopes for the blessed marriage, where we would both be walking with Jesus and serving Him one day, were getting quashed quickly. Christmas and New Year came and went and even though we had a lovely time, I was struggling inside, to the point where, in the first few days of January, I longed for and needed to go back to church, no matter what the cost would be. It was now that I felt my faith was really being put to the test. I felt God was saying to me, "Bruce are you serious about me and truly going to follow me, even if it costs you everything?" Inside, I heard myself saying, "Lord I can't or won't survive without you, I need you." It was then I decided no matter what the consequences, I was going back to church. I made the decision to go the Saturday night prayer meeting, which was not well received when I got home. Regardless, I went to church again on the Sunday morning, despite Lisa's feelings. Little did I realise that I was stepping into the fire and about to go through a truly testing time.

That afternoon, the tension was very high at home as I tried to explain why I needed to go back to church. By the Tuesday night, things had got very heated in the flat and my only option was to call Roy and explain to him what was going on and that I was desperate. He was great; he told me to come over and stay in his spare bedroom. After work the next day, I left a note for Lisa, explaining and pleading with her to understand why and how I needed to go back to church and that I needed Jesus. At the same time I tried to explain how I would still be committed to her and that she would have the priority of my time and attention and how our marriage could only improve with my faith. On that note, I went to a house group and when I got back things became unbearable. Lisa was 'on my case' like never before, and in her absolute desperation even trying to get her parents to talk sense into me, to give up all this so-called nonsense. It reached the point that I had to leave the flat; I was not able to cope and feared I would lose the plot with her. Roy had already said that if it got too much, to go back to his place. So that's what I did; I phoned Roy up and headed over to him. The Thursday was something else; at work and out of the blue, we were told that the removal company I worked for had gone into liquidation and as of tomorrow, we would all be out of a job. I then had to get the things they had kindly let me keep in storage and return them to the flat at the end of the day. My boss also kindly let me use a work van, which was much appreciated. I arranged to see my pastor that night also for advice.

What didn't help my situation was that Lisa had now messaged me by text, to say that she no longer wanted me at the flat and had literally thrown me out. Roy and Ros were brilliant; they opened their home and their family to me and had said to me that I was welcome to stay with them as long as needed. So that night, as I dropped off the stuff at the flat and picked up what I needed of my own belongings, I drove to West Kilbride to meet up with Pastor Bernie. We had a great chat and Pastor Bernie reassured me that God was faithful, and He would be with me through all that I was going through. He told me that God would honour me for making a stand on my faith and for Jesus. However, I wasn't expecting and a little taken aback by what he said next. He said if he had known me and Lisa before we got married, he would have told us not to get married; saying that he believed we were not meant to be together. As a new Christian, that wasn't something I was expecting to hear. After the meeting I headed back over to Roy's place, given that Lisa had made her feelings very clear.

The Friday was spent getting the company premises in order before it was seized by the administrators that afternoon. Thankfully, we still got paid in cash for that week, the expectation had been that we might not have even got that. So that Friday afternoon a group of us were sat in a local pub having a drink together, wondering what on earth had just happened (I was on soft drinks as I was now free from alcohol). I started laughing and one of the guys looked at me puzzled and said, "what are you laughing at?" I looked at him and said, "My life is like a Country and Western song just now; in a week I have lost my wife, my house and my job." I could laugh at this and I was not panicked or worried. I had a real sense of peace and joy and knew in my heart, that no matter what happens, God is in control. Looking back at the week before, when I had made the decision that I was serious, that I was going to go for God in all, no matter what, I never thought that I was going to be tested by fire as I was now. God was truly asking the exam but I serious for Him, even if it would cost me everything.

It was true; within a week I had lost my home, my marriage was in tatters and I had also lost my job. Jokingly, I thought if I had known that this was in the small print, I might have had second thoughts about signing on the dotted line! In all seriousness, even though I didn't know what the next step was to be, all my trust was in God; my very life was trusted in His hands and I knew I couldn't live without Him. My faith was to be tested but God was to show how faithful He truly is, and that He is in control. Lisa had made it very clear she did not want me at the flat, even though I had a hope for my marriage, and I did all that I could to show her that this was not what I wanted. I was doing what I could to get back on my feet; I registered homeless with the council and got my name down on the waiting list for housing. The Lord was faithful in that Roy gave me work with him in his forestry business, whilst also opening his home and family to me, encouraging me to stay as long as needed.

Roy said that he believed Jesus was asking him to open his home to me and I was treated by Roy and Ros like family. Over the coming weeks, Roy wasn't just a good friend and like a close brother to me, but he became a mentor and helped me in the early days of my walk with

Jesus. I was also part of an amazing church where I made many great friends, but was also treated like family, I was even part of a great men's mentoring program within the Bridge Church. God was faithful and I drew closer and closer to Jesus as He drew closer to me. I was so hungry for anything of Jesus and His Word. I continued to know and experience His love for me as each day passed. Yet I still felt the rejection from Lisa and I missed being loved and accepted and being intimate. But despite my feelings and what I was going through, I kept my eyes on Jesus and trusted in what He was allowing me to go through. The old me would have turned to drink and other women to get my needs and wants met.

But that me was gone; it was no more. Inside I was lonely and was hurting from the rejection from my wife, but God was teaching me a new way. One night, I was coming back with Roy from a men's retreat with the church at the Compass Christian Centre near Glenshee, when something that Roy shared with me really stuck. As he was driving, I remember him looking at me and saying "Bruce, Jesus has got someone for you in His timing, if it is not to be with Lisa. Trust Him!" I looked at Roy and thought "Yeah, right, it's easy for you to say when you have a blessed marriage and a wife that also loves Jesus". I was still very naive in many areas of my walk with Jesus at that time, and trust and patience were something I was still learning. As the weeks went by, I was growing in my walk and learning so much. My passion and love for Jesus was increasing and I remember sitting having dinner one evening with Roy and Ros, and I asked them what an evangelist was. This was something that was on my heart and wouldn't shift from my thoughts. Roy explained an evangelist was someone who shared Jesus with people with a raw and real passion, someone who was called by God to go and share the Gospel wherever and whenever God asked them to. I had a real stirring and a knowing inside that this was what I believed

God had put in my heart; that this was what God was asking of me. This is something that has only grown more and more inside me to this day. I shared with Roy and Ros that I felt this was what God was calling me to do and Roy encouraged me by saying he believed this also.

In the weeks I was staying with Roy I met up with Lisa once or twice to try and see if we could reconcile and rekindle our marriage, we met in public as she did not want me around at the flat. The meetings ended with more frustration than before they started, with Lisa putting unreasonable demands on me for any chance of us to get back together. I stood my ground, in that there would be no conditions put on my faith, at the same time trying to reassure her that my time with her would be a priority and my faith and time with Jesus would not clash with that. But we didn't get anywhere, and we parted company. I was still feeling the hurt and rejection from Lisa but I still had a hope that one day we would reconcile. I just kept my eyes on Jesus and my trust in Him. While out working planting trees one Friday, I felt Jesus speak to my heart, not an audible voice but a sense of truly knowing it was Him that was speaking. The only words that kept coming back to me again and again was "Move back to Edinburgh." Puzzled by this, I thought this did not make any sense. I had a good job, was part of a great church and part of an amazing men's mentoring programme, and I was soon to get my own place with the council. I thought my mind was just messing with me but the more I wrestled with this the more I just kept hearing "Move back to Edinburgh." This was absurd; the only place I would be able to go to was my parents and I would have no job, but the more I argued with this thought the more I got the same words again and again. I lost any peace I had inside me and I couldn't rest.

About this time, I felt it right to be thinking about moving out of Roy's house anyway. I thought about it and remembered I had a couple of old Regiment pals that lived in the area and who had offered to put me up if I needed a place to crash. That Friday night and Saturday I tried to call them, but I could not get hold of either of them. Every door I was trying to push open was getting slammed shut. I wrestled through the night trying to reason with the situation, but again the only words that kept coming to my mind, clear as anything, were, "Move back to Edinburgh. That Sunday morning, as soon as I finally surrendered my will to those words, a peace came upon me and a knowing that I truly knew was from God. I went downstairs. Roy was in the kitchen and he asked if he could have a chat. Before I could say anything, Roy explained that he felt it was probably time for me to look for somewhere else to stay, not that he was throwing me out or trying to put pressure on me, just that it was that time. I then went on to tell Roy that I was thinking the same thing myself and also that I felt Jesus was speaking to me about moving back to Edinburgh. I confided in Roy that I had been wrestling with this and how peace came upon me when I finally surrendered to it. Roy agreed with me; he explained that as I was talking, he got what he called a 'witness' in the spirit. Jesus had given Roy a word and an agreement that this was His plan. Then a real peace came over the both of us that we both knew this was definitely from Jesus.

Roy prayed with me and after church, I phoned dad and asked him if it would be ok to come back home. Dad being dad, compassionate and understanding said, "No problem son, what time will you be home? Looking forward to seeing you." I said that I would be home later that night, as I still had my spare key. After I had finished speaking to dad, I got my stuff together and, after some food with Roy and Ros, Roy drove me to Glasgow to get the train. We said our goodbyes and had a great chat and shared memories of the last few months, I arranged to come through and see them soon and went off to get my train. So here I was, heading back to

Edinburgh, without any idea of what was to happen next. I was certainly putting my faith to the test. I'll never forget standing there on Princes Street waiting for my bus and feeling at home and a peace and a joy came over me that I knew could only come from God. I had no job and no idea what the next step would be, but all I truly knew was that I was in God's hands; He was leading the way on the journey I was about to embark on. And I was home.

Chapter 11

I was now back at home, living with my parents and without a clue what the next step would be in my journey with Jesus. I registered with a driving agency I had been with before and got work straight away, while contacting Destiny Church in Gorgie, planning to visit it as I had been there previously, to a men's conference with Roy. One of the church staff named Beth got in touch straight away and invited me to come to the church for a coffee. She was part of the team who welcomed new people to the church and, after a coffee and chat about our journey and how we came to faith and so on, I really felt that this was the church God was telling me to attend. Before long I felt I was where I was meant to be and it felt like home. I made friends very quickly, becoming part of a lovely midweek house group, hosted by a lovely couple that lived near me. I also got involved with serving and became part of the 'tea and coffee team'.

There seemed to be domestic breakthrough, when Lisa got in contact and wanted to meet up; I was aware that we were due to have an IVF appointment at Glasgow's Royal Infirmary. This would be a one-and-only chance to obtain treatment on the NHS as Lisa was at the cut off age for it and there was no way we could afford it privately. We had started to go down this route as sadly I had a low sperm count and we had been unable to conceive naturally through our marriage. Children were the last thing on my mind right now, but I still had hopes for my marriage and I wanted to support Lisa, so we went along to our appointment. It was a very difficult and strained meeting, as the doctor gave us our options and emphasised that we needed to start the IVF as soon as possible, as any longer delay and we would reach out cut off time. I felt that I needed to stand my ground and make the decision; I was not ready to proceed until our marriage was sorted and stable, and I know we needed counselling and time to try and put our marriage back together.

After the appointment things were emotional. I felt as if I was being put under pressure, with guilt and condemnation; that I was robbing Lisa of a family and children because of my selfish choice not to commit to IVF, losing our opportunity to one last chance on the NHS. As much as I was trying not to get upset, I was tearful but I just knew I had to stand my ground. I was in no way ready or prepared to commit to trying for a family until my marriage had been worked at. As a result, we missed our opportunity for treatment and in her anger, Lisa stopped any contact with me for a period of time. Part of me felt that she had only entertained the possibility of us getting back together so that she could have this IVF treatment and have a child, something I knew she so desperately wanted. At the same time, I knew in my heart that it was not right to go down that route until I knew our marriage was on a path of recovery and knowing we had a future together.

Not long after this, I heard an amazing sermon on Godly forgiveness, preached by my pastor. When he spoke, I knew that God was speaking to me directly. It spoke so much to me that forgiveness doesn't benefit the person you are forgiving, but it benefits you yourself; it frees you up from carrying the bitterness, anger and resentment. It didn't mean that reconciliation was possible in a situation, but it did allow you to be free in your heart. Forgiveness was not one-off event, but something you would have to keep doing over and over again. I learned we cannot forgive someone with our own strength, but only through the strength of Jesus. Vitally, I learned that Jesus gives us the strength, the compassion and the ability to keep on going and forgiving someone. I had to apply what was being spoken to my feelings towards Lisa; it was only in Jesus that I could walk free from all my emotional baggage.

I loved how each day Jesus would draw close to me and speak to me in amazing ways, not in an audible voice but in a sense of feeling His love and presence and in how His word jumped out at me as I read the bible. Listening to worship songs, I just knew He was there, and He was speaking to me. One particular weekend I felt more and more the call of an evangelist ever so clearly on my heart and it wasn't going away. I happened to be online and a guy from the Destiny Church, an evangelist by the name of John Lawson, was offering a couple of free tickets to a conference at Westerhailes Baptist Church that Saturday. I messaged John and shared brief account of how I had come to the faith and how I felt that I also had the call. I told him that I would be interested in one of the tickets as money was very tight just then. John called me about an hour later and we had a great chat; he told me that a ticket would be at the reception for me and he looked forward to meeting me. On the morning of the conference I had accepted the fact that my marriage may be well and truly over and I said to God that morning, "It's just me and you now God, I don't want anyone or need anyone else. My life is yours to use me any way you want to." I had a feeling of His presence upon me and in time I felt God was saying to me, " Son, you have no idea what I'm about to do in your life because I love you."

I went to the conference and met John and a colleague from the ministry he was involved with, a gentleman called Renton. Before the conference started, I found a seat at the front and John and Renton introduced themselves, sharing a little about their pasts, which was quite an eye opener and interesting. Having come from backgrounds of football thuggery and criminality, they told me how Jesus had got hold of them and transformed them and called them to become evangelists and share the Gospel. I loved how God took the misfits, delinquents and rejects of this world and used them for His glory. John and Renton explained that this conference was called 'Release' and it was designed to help equip and teach people to share their faith and their story confidently and how to share Jesus with people. After the first session we were all encouraged to split into groups, introduce ourselves and discuss our own experiences of faith and how we had come to it.

Accordingly, we broke into small groups, sat in circles and started to talk. That's when she caught my attention. It was nothing sexual or lustful that made her get my attention, it was the way and the power behind what she was sharing. I was certainly in no place or even interested in meeting anyone else; Jesus had my whole focus and attention. I just remember, as she was sharing her life and experiences of how she had come to faith, and the difficulty in the divorce she was going through, I could see JESUS in her eyes and had His hand upon her life. I saw the same peace upon her that I first saw on Roy when he was telling me about his life. I could relate with her pain of rejection from someone you loved, who didn't accept what you had become in Jesus. When she was talking, I would get eye contact with her.

Again, it was nothing flirtatious or sexual; I honestly saw Jesus through her eyes. I was able to share my own journey and how I was going through a hard marriage breakup. I did feel uncomfortable at one point, when I could feel a young lady almost opposite me looking at me in a flirtatious way. But I certainly was not interested and I was not trying to give off any signals that I may have been interested, as that was the last thing I wanted to do; it felt awkward and uncomfortable, especially as Jesus was teaching me a new way to walk. It was a small world: at lunchtime I met a gentleman I knew and hadn't seen 1995. His name was Keith and he was one of the instructors when I went through the Prince's Trust Volunteers Course. I had no idea he was a believer, but it was so nice to see him again.

At lunch chatting to someone, the young lady who had been looking at me and the woman in whom I had seen Jesus, came and sat at our table. I was talking with the guy next to me about the church I attended and who my pastor was, when this woman lent over, apologised for interrupting and asked where this church was, as she had overheard me and heard a lot about my pastor. I explained where Destiny Church was and that my pastor was the lead pastor there. I thought nothing more of the conversation and the afternoon conference sessions proceeded. A gentleman named Billy got up and said he was from Edinburgh City Mission, involved with Outreach on Friday nights, where volunteers from different churches and denominations would go to the Cowgate area of Edinburgh and provide tea, coffee and literature and chat to local revellers about Jesus, if they wanted to. Billy asked anyone who might be interested in this Outreach to speak with him after the conference. It certainly had my interest and I felt a real desire to get involved with this kind of ministry. After the conference I had a great chat with Billy and arranged to meet up with him sometime for a coffee. Then I felt Jesus tell me to go up to the woman I had met at the conference and invite her to Destiny the following day. I went up to her and introduced myself properly and invited her to come Destiny with the friends she had come to the conference with, Her name was Julie and we said our goodbyes and I headed home. Julie came to church the next day with a few of her friends, and she also brought along her five-year-old son Lawson.

After the service, we had a good chat and got to know each other a little, sharing the stories of the journeys we had been on. A friendship started, but there was no romantic flirtation. Neither of us were in a place or even interested in meeting anyone. As time went on, I became more and more involved with the church and seeking Jesus. John became a mentor to me, and we would meet regularly for a coffee and a chat. I got to know Billy very as well and we would meet for a brew, becoming good friends. I was very interested in getting involved with the Outreach in Edinburgh's Cowgate on Friday nights and Billy was helping me, making sure that I was ready and able to be involved. Sometimes, Julie would visit her family in Edinburgh, and would come along to Destiny where we would have a chat and a coffee after the service. She was part of a mentoring program with the same ministry as John Lawson, and so we had a common interest in Jesus and our faith, which gave us plenty to chat about. Around this time, I felt that Jesus was asking me to try again with Lisa and work at my marriage. Surprisingly, when I got in contact with her, Lisa agreed to meet and we chatted. She agreed to try, and was a little more accepting of my faith, but somewhat reluctantly. We agreed to seek marriage counselling and I travelled at the weekends to see her. However, it was difficult and whilst I was trying my best, it wasn't long before we were back to where we were before. Lisa was placing demands upon me over my faith and the marriage counselling sessions became emotional, difficult and very strained.

When I returned to Edinburgh after my weekends visiting Lisa in Ayrshire, I felt tearful, emotional and guilty for having to try and justify my relationship with Jesus. It was as it had been before I moved out the first time. Each Sunday night heading back to Edinburgh, I cried out to God, "When is it going to change between me and Lisa?" I had hoped that she would come to know Jesus as I had done, but I also had to accept that she may never want to know Him. This was a really difficult and testing time and I truly didn't know how much longer I could carry on trying. I just knew that God was asking this of me, but my love for Lisa was being strained to the point I don't want to do this anymore; I was struggling to keep trying and being put through the emotional heartache and hurt. It was getting to the point where I was being accused of all manner of things, accused of not trying and it became heated and ugly, to the point of me almost completely losing it in a fit of rage. I had to get myself out of the firing line and I remember one night, walking the streets of Glasgow, crying my eyes out and calling out to Jesus in sheer desperation, pleading, "How long is this going to continue?" I was telling Jesus with all my heart that I trying so hard, but I didn't know how much more I could take.

It got to the point when Lisa told me she didn't love this 'man of God' I was trying to be; she wanted this nonsense to stop and wanted her old husband back. It came to a head, something had to change and a decision had to be made. I was praying to Jesus to give me strength and help me, as I knew deep down that my heart wasn't in it anymore; I needed Jesus to get through this meeting with Lisa, but it was a disaster; it was painful, emotional and a real struggle. It became very heated and got to the point when it was literally her or God, as we repeated the same battles as before. Then I made the decision, right or wrong; I just knew I was too worn down and broken by it all. My heart was not in it anymore and I knew that the love I had for Lisa was gone. I still had love in my heart for her; I cared for her, but I felt like a beaten dog and knew I was no longer in love with her as my wife. I said that enough was enough; I was done and I wasn't doing this anymore; that the marriage was over.

It was horrendous when I finally plucked up the courage and headed out through the door. It was tearful and there was shouting, tears and anger, but I knew I had to walk for my own sanity and mental health. As I sat on the train back to Edinburgh, tearful and emotional and reflecting on all that had just happened, I felt His peace come over me. I believe His hand was upon me, affirming that He was in control. I felt His presence envelop me. I knew there and then that my marriage was over and that was the last time I have ever seen Lisa in person to this day. Looking back, could I have tried harder or done things differently? The answer is absolutely! At the time, I believe I gave it all that I could and put my whole heart into trying, but it came to a point where a man can only take so much. I very likely did a lot of things wrong, but I also can't live in the past of regrets and sorrow. The only thing could do now was move on and start putting my life back together. It was just me and God now and I was content for that to be for the rest of my life. I had given Him everything and it was in my heart to serve Him in any way He called me to. I had no idea of the journey God was going to take me.

The door now opened for me to get involved with Friday night Outreach on the Cowgate with Edinburgh City Mission. We would meet in the back hall of St Colomba's Church at the top of the Royal Mile. A whole load of us from different churches would gather, all with a passion to share our faith. After a time of prayer, Billy and a gentleman called Paul who headed up the Outreach, would take the team down into the Cowgate, known as the underbelly of Edinburgh City's old town. There, we split into two teams and set up a table with tea and coffee for passers-by, and literature for anyone interested. We would be a friendly presence and chatted with people who stopped for a tea or a coffee. Each Friday night was different, and I would have some amazing chats with people about Jesus, about life and all manners of things. It was a great opportunity to be bold with my faith and to share my journey with others. I felt a real calling to the Outreach work I was doing.

Some nights, I would happily just make tea and coffee for tipsy revellers. There was the odd instance with someone getting a little out of order, but nothing I couldn't handle. The Outreach had a really positive influence in the area; it was welcomed by the police, the bouncers and the regulars we who stopped at the table. The Outreach didn't preach at people, but it gave an opportunity for people to come and speak to us and we could then open up to them about Jesus and our faith. It was a steep learning curve for me, in at the deep end and sharing my faith, but I really enjoyed it. I was in contact with Julie and a friendship really started to blossom between us. As I was now becoming involved with the same mentoring program as she was, we had the connection of something we were both involved with. Through John Lawson, I now started to become involved with Avanti ministries to start training as an evangelist, as I felt this was God's call on my life. The mentoring program was designed to equip you to step out and effectively share the Gospel. This was done with bible and practical training, with the aid of a mentor to whom you would be accountable and who would assist you to work through a program of bible study and paperwork. The idea was to train someone in fulfilling the role of an evangelist, with opportunities for Outreach and mission work through the ministry itself, here in the U.K or even abroad when opportunities arose. The ministry was headed by a gentleman called Tony Anthony, who had quite a testimony to tell himself; a sincere and humble man who loved Jesus and had a passion to share the Gospel wherever and whenever an opportunity arose.

As I got to know Julie as a dear friend, I also got to know her son, Lawson. God gave me a father's love for him, especially as his biological father was not in his life at that time. I was to experience a glimpse of God's heart and love for this little boy and we soon became real buddies. In time, I started to have feelings for Julie and an attraction sparked; both of us realised that we had feelings for each other, but we knew we couldn't be anything more than friends, especially as she was just coming through a divorce and I hadn't even started divorce proceedings. It was around this time that I went to see a divorce lawyer who was recommended by a friend, to start the process of a divorce. I wanted to find out where I stood and to explain what I was wanting out of a divorce, which was nothing materialistic I didn't want anything other than to just move on with my life.

During the meeting I explained my situation; Lisa owned the flat and I owned the car which she still had, but that I had no issues with that as I was willing to give her the car. My lawyer explained that it was an easy enough divorce case, especially as we had no kids and that if Lisa was in agreement to what he drafted, our divorce could be as early as a year from when I officially moved out of the flat the previous January. By mutual agreement, a divorce could take place with a minimum of a year's separation. If she was to make it difficult and contest it, then my other option was to wait a minimum of 2 years of separation and I could then divorce without her consent. My hope was for the one-year and then we could both just move on with our lives. Lisa made it completely difficult and did not agree, even stating to my Lawyer that we had trying to get together again throughout the year. All was not lost, as my Lawyer told me that by his calculations, the period spent trying together only added about a month and a half onto the minimum one-year divorce, if she agreed. But Lisa was still fighting it, and I was looking at having to wait a minimum of 2 years. I did find this frustrating, as I just wanted to get on with my life. Was I enjoying this? No! Does God hate divorce? Yes! But I also believe that God allows divorce, albeit there are consequences. At the end of the day, I just wanted to get on with life and knew that in time I would be able to do so, but I was also aware of the implications divorce brings.

With the expectation of waiting two years, I got on with life as best I could. I soon realised that I was in love with Julie, but I knew that we were not able to have a future as a couple until I was divorced. Yes, we could have hooked up like everyone else does, and no one would think anything of it. But we were accountable to God as we professed to walk with Jesus, and we had to walk the walk if we talked the talk, especially as we both had a calling and a hope to be used by God in Evangelism. Hypocrisy was something we couldn't afford. We both had hope for a future together, but we knew we could only be friends and we submitted that before God. I was being tested every day and being put through the fire with the need to show forgiveness. Every day I had to bring Lisa before the Lord and ask Him to give me the strength to continue to forgive her in every area of my life, especially the fact that she still had some hold and control over me by being difficult with the divorce. I had to forgive her continuously throughout the day, every day.

I was really tested when I realised that the only things I held of any value were the medals I had earned for my service in the military and going to war. I had accidentally left these at the flat when I moved out. I got in contact with Lisa to ask for them back, but she coldly let me know she had binned them. I was certainly put to the test by this. My first reaction was one of sheer anger and bitterness, as the medals had held great sentimental value for me. I seeked the Lord on this, and in my time of quiet with Him I believed that Jesus spoke to my heart about it. I believe He was telling me that these medals were just metal and ribbon and held no eternal value. I also believe He was asking me if I loved these medals over Him and challenging me that they had become an idol. It was then I realised that, you know what? That that's just what they really were! Just a bit of tin and ribbon. I could get them replaced if I needed to and that's when they lost any value to me and I let it go. At the end of the day I know what I had done, and I didn't need medals on my chest to tell me that. So, I let it go and chose to forgive Lisa for throwing them away and anyway, perhaps part of me couldn't blame her for doing that. I gave the whole situation over to Jesus and allowed Him to take that issue off my heart.

I was still very much involved with Outreach on Friday nights in Edinburgh; serving teas and coffees on a Sunday at church and working hard driving trucks during the week, but I still had struggles, like anyone else. I was still battling bouts of depression; this was something the Lord had not freed me from even though He had healed me of alcoholism. I prayed every day to be freed of depression and even though God had not freed me from it, I trusted Him all the same. I was very involved with the mentoring program and making good ground with the bible and theological study coursework. I spoke regularly to my mentors, John Lawson and Tina, and kept regular accounts with them with on how I was getting on.

One activity on the mentoring program was to write out your full testimony, everything of significance. I had already done this earlier and I ended up with nearly twenty to thirty pages. I found this to be a very emotional exercise, but yet a healing one too, as I believed it had allowed the Lord to visit areas of my life that needed healing. The next exercise was to condense your written testimony to two or three pages. Then the final exercise of writing this testimony was to get it down to one A4 page, the idea being to help us when we gave our testimony verbally. Having my testimony written out in full, then two or three pages and finally one page was to aid me in when I only had thirty minutes or ten minutes or even five minutes to speak. Tony Anthony helped me greatly with this, which was very much appreciated. Next, we were to practise sharing our testimony with someone, being assigned only ten minutes and also five minutes to speak. This was to train us to go on Outreach and to be prepared for any timeframe given. To keep within that time was a discipline we were trained to keep and was very important.

On speaking to Tony at the later part of the year, an opportunity came for me to go to Moldova on a week's mission to a bible school there, and to shadow an evangelist team teaching out there. I was even given the opportunity to share my testimony and it was an amazing experience. The pastor and bible teacher at the school really impressed me in that he preached to His congregation not only in Romanian and English, but also in Russian. While in Moldova we got to visit a few orphanages and to see how locals lived there. It was a real eye-opener and a life changing experience, seeing the poverty and yet the love of God and hospitality these precious people showed; they didn't have much, but they shared what they had with the team. It was amusing that, because of my build and shaved head, many of the Moldovans thought I was Ukranian and looked like a Ukranian soldier. I even nearly had trouble getting out of the country at the airport. I was being interrogated at customs by quite a stern looking Moldovan policeman asking me all sorts of questions and closely inspecting me and at my passport.

It was certainly a great experience in Moldova and one that I would never forget. I felt that Jesus was putting in my heart a love for broken men, stuck in addictions, with mental health issues, depression, PTSD, veterans and soldiers. I felt the Lord was preparing me to one day reach out to men who have a similar background to mine. Although I was spending a lot of time with Julie and had a real hope for a future for the two of us, we both still knew that our friendship couldn't be anything more than that. Yes, we had a kiss and a cuddle now and then, but that was all and we knew we weren't honouring God in doing that and had to stop. Our attention was being distracted from what God was asking of us and redirected to each other. Julie was the stronger one in pointing out that we were being distracted. There was still no change from Lisa in agreeing to the divorce, and I found this frustrating. God was still using me on the Outreach on Friday nights, but I still struggled with loneliness; a longing to be truly loved with someone and a desire to be intimate, but I kept giving these thoughts over to Jesus and in His strength, I was able to keep my eyes on Him. I found the more I drew closer to Him to seek the affirmation I needed the more He drew closer to me.

It was after New Year in the January of 2011 that Julie contacted me over the 'phone, to tell me that she believed the Lord was telling her that we were to have no more contact; that we weren't honouring Him that He wanted us both to be able to focus on what He was calling both of us to do for Him. Julie explained that we were to absolutely have no more contact with each other, indefinitely. When I came off the 'phone I cried my heart out; yes we were friends, but I also knew that I loved Julie and had a hope that we would one day have a future. I remember crying out to God and asking Him why He didn't understand that I had a love for Julie, but now she was gone from my life. It was very difficult; I felt rejection again. I felt lonely and for a while I struggled to turn completely to God. Totally broken, I surrendered everything again to Him, but it was a battle to completely surrender all hope of a future with Julie over to Him. In rebellion, I held onto a glimmer of hope for Julie. I would surrender for the full two years of separation for my divorce to proceed.

Over the next few weeks in my brokenness and struggles, God still used me. I had now become involved with a Christ-centred help group called 'Celebrate Recovery.' This was run at Destiny by a lovely couple; Dennis and Sharon. This group aimed to help those with addictions, hang ups and brokenness in their lives. Let's face it, everyone needs help of some kind and has issues and hang ups in their lives. What was unique about this help group was that Jesus actually was the higher power. It was a real blessing in my life to be involved in and this, and I found that God used me in my own brokenness to help others coming to the group. It was also around his time that God brought a very dear man into my life who was to become a close friend and much needed mentor in my life. Not only that, he became a spiritual father to me and God gave him a father's love for me, and a son's love for me towards him.

This man's name was Tim; a very gentle and mighty man of God and an American missionary. It was through Tim and another gentleman like me called Bruce, that I became involved with their ministry Outreach. They headed a ministry called 'JOHN 3:7', an evangelistic ministry that took them out onto the streets carrying big yellow signs with 'JOHN 3:7' written on them. These boards were a focal point that would attract people to them. Those with the boards would stand on the streets and people would be drawn to them and ask what is 'JOHN 3:7' which is a scripture from the bible. This would then be an opening to be able to share Jesus with people. It was a great ministry; I felt privileged to be involved with it and we would normally stand up and down the Royal

Mile in Edinburgh on a Thursday Night and Saturday Night.

The ministry supported Street Church on Hunter's Square, just off the Royal Mile, a local church which took church and Jesus to the streets - to people who would never set foot in a church. I loved the fact that, at my most broken, God could use me mightily in service for Him to reach out to others in how God loves them. I spent many hours with Tim ministering on the capital's streets, yet at the same time being ministered to by God through Tim. I finally came to a place of complete surrender and acceptance that there was not a future or even any glimpse of a hope of a future with Julie in my life. When I had completely accepted that I would never see Julie again, God moved in my life and I would never have dreamed of what was next about to happen in my life and the journey God was about to take me on.

Chapter 12

Two days after I had completely surrendered
my own will with regards to Julie, she got in
contact. She explained that she was coming to
Edinburgh and that she had felt God had told
her that it was ok for her to contact me. We
arranged to meet for a coffee, and I was quite
excited in the thought of seeing her. When we
met, she explained what had been happening
with her and how she felt that the Lord was
clear on her having no more contact with me,
indefinitely. Julie told me how difficult it had
been for her, but she had accepted it and from
day one had laid aside her own desires in order
to be obedient to God. She told me that it had
been forty days of having no contact before
God finally spoke to her and told her she was
able to contact me. Reflecting on my own
journey, it was clear that I had been reluctant to
suppress my own desires towards Julie in order
to share that same obedience to God. I could
see in Julie's eyes for the first time, how open

and vulnerable she was. She explained that God was guiding her to meet with me to chat, but to be open to the fact that I might not want to meet or, even worse, reject her. I may even have met someone else. All the while, she was fighting back the tears, looking at me and telling me that she was totally in love with me; I could see the apprehension in her eyes, waiting to see what my response would be. I knew I truly loved her and there and then, I fell in love with her even more. I told her I loved her too and the both of us were trying to hold back the tears and the snot.

People must have been looking at the two of us and wondering what on earth we were doing. We both had real hope for the future, and after that meeting doors seemed to suddenly open. We knew at this point we could still only be friends, but Julie was worth waiting for. That same week I had a message out of the blue from my Lawyer, saying that Lisa had come around and agreed to the divorce. My Lawyer was now in the process of finalising the paperwork and it should only matter of weeks before the divorce came through and I would finally be free. At the same time, an opportunity arose to go on an Outreach with Tony Anthony and Billy from Edinburgh City Mission. Billy and I accompanied Tony on a week of visits around Scotland, where Tony was speaking. We visited a couple of Prisons, a school, a rehabilitation centre and a few churches. I was given the opportunity to share my testimony in front of quite a few large crowds, as well as a few small gatherings. To share my testimony in a prison was something else. I was totally at peace, sharing my journey in front of a bunch of prisoners, that included murderers, hard men and professional criminals, but I had a boldness to share my love of Jesus and how He had stepped into the mess of my life and transformed me from the inside out. A couple of the prisoners who heard me were veterans themselves; they told me how they had struggled in civilian life and had fallen in with the wrong crowd or been involved in some dodgy things which led them to being sent down. I had a real heart for these guys and had no difficulty in sharing with them. I was very touched when a couple of them told me that they were really moved by what I had shared with them.

The Outreach was a real eye opener and a real blessing to be part of. I was even asked to share with a high school class of teenagers. I actually found that more difficult and nerve-racking than sharing with a bunch of hardened prisoners. I found the one thing with teenagers; they see authenticity and see through hypocrisy. I can't remember exactly what I shared with them but was again touched to hear them say also they were moved by my honesty and what I had shared. The strange thing is that every time I had shared and still share, I never know exactly what I'm going to say, as I believe that I allow Jesus to speak through me; I try to always be open and brutally honest. Something Tony shared with me that still has an impact today, was when he said, "Bruce, never lose that vulnerability you have when you speak." That's exactly what I try and allow myself to be whenever I'm given the privilege to share my faith; to be open and vulnerable and with that, I generally get tearful and emotional when I share in public; something I embrace as a gift not a weakness.

After the Outreach I recalled having said to a friend. "God would never use me to speak in prisons and schools!" I had to laugh; it made me realise to be careful what you say, because God may just do what you claim He won't. I was also asked to share my testimony at one of the Celebrate Recovery evenings. Again, I didn't know what I was going to share, but I believe that God touched the hearts of many who came to that evening. Around this time, I introduced Julie to my dear friend Tim, my mentor and spiritual father. As I spent time with Tim, he encouraged me, telling me how far he had seen me come and how much he could see Jesus at work in my life. Another Outreach opportunity with Tony and Billy came around again, on the west coast of Scotland where I visited another couple of prisons and was able to share my testimony with the inmates.

This was a really good opportunity to get to know Tony better and to connect with him. In one of our chats I told Tony that I believed the Lord had been speaking to me, and I believed that God was calling me to be an evangelist and missionary here in the UK, not overseas. It felt as if the Lord was giving me His heart for the lost and broken of this nation. But I also believed that God was asking me, first and foremost, to get to know Him more intimately. I was aware of how we could so easily become more concerned over what we were doing for God rather than actually getting to know Him more intimately. An opportunity came for Julie to go to French Guiana on a mission trip and while she was away, I took time off work for a few days to look after her son Lawson. This was a real blessing and an opportunity to bond with him. We had a great time and I took him on all the sights of Edinburgh, which he loved.

I had a call from my Lawyer to tell me that all the paperwork had gone through and was being finalised; it wouldn't be long until my divorce certificate would come through. About this time, I started to make plans to move to Newtonmore, where Julie lived. She was a childminder and it was turning out that over the summer she would have enough kids under her care for me to be able to work alongside her. Friends who lived nearby had also offered for me to rent a spare room. Julie and I had a real hope for the future, and we knew we wanted to be together and believed that as we honoured God, then He would honour us. We truly believed that God, in His own time, was allowing us to have a future together and we both knew that at the right time, we would be married. We believed God's hand was in this and He was bringing us together. In early June I moved to Edinburgh and in the same week I got my divorce certificate officially signed and I moved to Newtonmore.

That summer I worked with Julie as an assistant childminder; with the kids we had in our care it certainly was a challenge but a rewarding one. Because we knew that one day we were to be married, we chose to use the purity rings we had bought for each other to be our wedding rings. Julie's engagement ring was to be made from the diamond of her nanna's engagement ring and the shaft of her mum's engagement ring, from her birthfather who she had lost at a very young age. God was involved in every little detail of this. We had bought the purity rings for each other when we were friends, as a sign of waiting and being pure for each other, in the hope of a future one day. Julie's ring had inscribed on it: 'True love waits' and my ring was inscribed with one of my favourite scriptures, Solomon chapter six, verse three: ' I am my beloved's and my beloved is mine." I was now living in Newtonmore making a new life for myself and now divorced, but I was yet to officially ask Julie to marry me.

With the help of Lawson, I arranged for Julie to meet us up 'The Glen', leaving notes for her explaining where to go, as we went ahead of her. Eventually, Julie was led to the riverbank where Lawson and I were waiting for her. With Lawson in charge of the engagement ring, I got down on one knee and asked Julie to marry me. She said yes and finally, after longing and waiting and hoping, we were now officially engaged to be married and Jesus as was at the centre; we knew if it hadn't been for Jesus, we would not have been together. As we had both come from radical pasts, with a series of relationships and a failed marriage each, in order to please Jesus, we decided to do this right! We would wait until our wedding night before any intimacy and we wouldn't live together until we were married. We both wanted to keep ourselves pure for each other and knew that we were each worth waiting for. As summer was coming to an end, numbers for Childminding were to soon decrease, so I started to look at options for work and at the same time looking for another place to stay as our friend's spare room was no longer available.

Again, this is where I believe that God honoured and came through for us. An ex-RAF physical training instructor named Laurie owned the local hostel and chatting with him, he generously offered to rent me a room at the hostel for a special monthly rate. The only drawback was that I might have to bed or room-hop depending on the bookings that came in, but I was more than flexible, and it was only to be for a few months, as Julie and myself planned our wedding. It was apparent that Julie was seeking the Lord for guidance on our wedding date; He came through and answered her. We planned a very short engagement, as we were in no doubt and had confirmation in many ways that this marriage came from the Lord and we were brought together by Him for a reason. As Julie was looking at the calendar, the Lord put it in her heart that our wedding day was to be 12th November 2011. Significantly, this date was the anniversary of my enlistment into the RAF Regiment and also the anniversary of the commitment to Jesus given by a dear friend, who plays a very key role in both mine and Julie's life. She was also chosen to be a bridesmaid. It was also very significant to my wife, as it the date when her previous marriage was completely was destroyed, but here we were, with God showing Julie how he is completely restoring and giving her more than she had lost. So, this was a really significant date for us both, and God's hand was truly upon it. As we both had evangelistic hearts, our plan was to use this as an opportunity for an evangelistic crusade for all our friends and family to hear about Jesus. But it was also to be a testimony of how God has brought two broken lives together and made them one on a new journey.

It was just about this time that the Lord was to really test how much were we prepared to sacrifice and put others needs before our own. Lawson's biological father was to come back into his life and it was to be a real test of how much we really wanted others to have the Lord's heart, even though it would become very uncomfortable for each of us. Julie and I had prayed for God's heart for the lost and broken of this world (as we still do) but He was about to really test us in this. God was teaching me a new way to love others, but He was also teaching me how to start loving myself and who He created me to be. For too long, I had carried hatred for myself and anger and resentment for my choices and actions; in how I acted and reacted with people and, more importantly, how frustrated I would get with myself for allowing people to walk all over me for years. God was teaching me to let go, to embrace my emotions and sensitivity and gentleness, that these were a gift from Him, not a weakness that I had taught myself to believe in the past. God was showing me to wear my heart on my sleeve and was giving me freedom to be open about anything and to talk about anything to anyone. God was allowing me to have a compassion and an empathy for others I never knew before, it allowed me to become vulnerable in front of people and to be able to show a soft side that people could connect with.

One of the blessings of God revealing to me a gentle and sensitive side, was to be able to hear from Him in ways I never thought possible. But the gentleness God had given me made me more susceptible to being hurt emotionally, which in turn would direct me to leaning on Him more and more. On the outside I may have looked tough, physically strong, with muscles, tattoos and a shaved head. Underneath I was really a gentle soul; this was all new to me and I was still learning. Jokingly, Julie always tells me I look tough on the outside but really am just a big gentle teddy bear. Adrian, Lawson's birth father, came into our lives. He was not in a good place and we certainly didn't have to have him in our lives, but God gave me a real heart for Him. I felt the Lord ask me to help get him accommodation at the hostel, and to help him get a job at the Glen Hotel (where he had once worked before). I did this gladly, with a genuine desire to help him. I was also applying for a job at the Glen Hotel, as there was no driving work nearby; I was not a proud man and would happily put my hand to anything. Funnily enough, Chris and Kim who owned the hotel gave Adrian a job as a chef and they also took me on to work in housekeeping and the kitchen, with waiting and even helping out with maintenance if needed. I was delighted and happy to work in any department.

It was good that Lawson was able to have Adrian back in his life and I did everything I could to encourage and support their relationship. I could truly put my hand on heart and say I counted Adrian as a dear friend and really cared for him. It is only God that could do that and all that had happened. People in the village must have thought we were mad for what we were doing, but then they thought we were nuts anyway, because of our faith and love for Jesus. One thing for sure; this was a real opportunity to demonstrate what Jesus's radical grace, love and forgiveness really looked like in the flesh. It certainly wasn't easy and there were days when both Julie and I would really be tested, asking ourselves 'really?' But this was Jesus's heart for Adrian working through us, and not of our own doing or strength. At one point I was working alongside Adrian every day in the hotel and actually sharing a bunk with Him in the hostel at night; you certainly couldn't make this stuff up!

As time went on, Julie and I were busy planning for the wedding. We didn't have a lot of money and we certainly weren't planning a big expensive wedding, the venue was to be my old church building, Destiny Church in Gorgie, of Edinburgh. The church building was an old cinema and bingo hall and it would be a great location for our wedding. My old pastor, Pastor Peter Anderson, agreed to marry us and we asked him to incorporate the whole Gospel message into our wedding. We decided to go for afternoon tea and cakes idea for the wedding breakfast, as we weren't wanting a big Reception. For us, our wedding was mainly about sharing the story of how God had brought two broken lives together in marriage, and of His Love, His Redemption and His Restoration of two lives in the blessings of His Covenant of marriage, with the ones we loved and cared about. The Lord even provided Julie's wedding dress, from what she had got from the sale of the watch inherited from her birth father. It was through God that Julie's birth father brought Julie's beautiful wedding dress; another example. of God's fatherliness, involved in the most intricate of details of our lives. Once we were married our plan was for just the two of us to have a small honeymoon at Crieff Hydro for a few days and then we would hire a self-catering house for a week and have Lawson with us and a real celebration of our new family together. I felt it right that I also asked Lawson to be my best man. Because of his age he couldn't carry out the legal duties of that role, but he would be with me upfront during the ceremony. My friend Roy kindly offered to be a witness to sign the wedding certificate. Our dear friend Izza and Yvonne along with my niece Kirsty were bridesmaids and even Julie's childhood 'Hollywood friend' as we called her, flew in from Los Angeles to be a bridesmaid. We all travelled to Edinburgh a couple of days before the big day.

On the Thursday before we were married, Ian McCormack was sharing his testimony at Destiny Church. He is a pastor and an evangelist with a mighty testimony of how he died, went to hell and heaven but God brought him back.

A New Zealander and a very humble man, it was inspiring to listen to him again and I got an opportunity to chat with Him a little. Before the wedding Lawson and I stayed at my mum and dad's and had Adrian stay as well. He had kindly offered to help with the catering, as we were pretty much arranging it ourselves. Everything was coming together, and it didn't feel strange at all that my soon-to-be wife's ex-husband was not only going to be at the wedding but would be helping with the arrangements. I thought nothing of it and counted him as a dear friend - again this was testimony of God's love and grace in action.

When the day of the wedding came and Lawson and I got to the church in full kilts and jackets, I was starting to get nervous, but Lawson calmed me and gave me advice. So many people we knew and loved had come to celebrate our special day with us and it was overwhelming to see the numbers of people who cared for us both to be there. I remember standing at the front of the church waiting for Julie to arrive; Pastor Peter was chatting with me to ease my nerves and Lawson was doing a great job of best man. I will never forget how beautiful Julie looked when she came down the aisle with stepdad Kenny, and as she arrived next to me, I was finally able to turn and look at her. The service was unbelievable, and Pastor Peter shared an amazing message on God's covenant of marriage and as promised, shared the Gospel message; it was like a Billy Graham crusade with the bonus of a wedding. It had been our intent that we wanted the importance of Jesus to be shared at our wedding and how it was only because of Him that everyone was there that day to see us be married.

It was great to have the freedom to worship Jesus during our wedding, even having my hands raised to Him in love and adoration during the worship music, not caring of what others may think but to simply adore Him. Besides that, I was battling not to get tearful with emotion during the service. The wedding photographer was brilliant, he was able to capture the whole wedding with both photos and a video that we can cherish always.

He took one photo that Julie and I had not realised was being taken; a black and white snap, taken from behind with a close-up of us both holding hands during the ceremony. It's my absolute favourite and sums up the whole journey we had both been on leading up to that day. It speaks of God's ultimate love for us both; how he brought two broken and shattered lives together in union, the covenant and blessing of His plan and purpose of marriage. We were now one, united by Jesus who is at the centre of our lives, our marriage and family, and how this was not possible without Him. It speaks of Hope and Promise and commitment and Faithfulness but most importantly of His ultimate and unconditional love.

We had a really blessed honeymoon at Crieff Hydro, just the two of us, able to could give each other completely focussed attention and later, a great time having Lawson with us and being able to spend time together as a new family. We settled into married life as a family unit very quickly in Newtonmore. I love how God gives the desires of our hearts to those who truly love and seek Him. I was not only blessed with the love of my life and a son I loved as my own, but I now had a dog, a black and tan King Charles Cavalier, called Humbug. He was a man's dog and we bonded and were inseparable; I had always wanted a dog to truly call my own and Humbug was that gift from God. As much as I loved Julie, Lawson and Humbug, it was quite an adjustment to get used to. I wasn't just a husband and a father, I was now a Christian husband and a Christian father, and it was to Jesus I was answerable. I was thrown in at the deep end with a steep learning curve, and certainly one where I made many mistakes along the way. Even though Julie and I had been married before this was completely new and different in every way, and we were both new and learning at this. We both had baggage that we brought to the marriage, that we still needed to deal with. I did not want to let Julie down, or fail her and Lawson, and I put a lot of pressure on myself.

I had never raised a child before and didn't know how to truly love as a Christian parent and husband; I was very much a student as was Julie. From her own past journey, I believe she struggled to truly show love at times, and I found this hard. Because of my own past, I would come across as being on the defensive when I was asked something by Julie, feeling as if I was being accused of something. The principle that I stood on was that no matter what, I am married and committed to Julie. I think the new transition put a lot of stress on me; I now had a wife and son who I was not only responsible for financially, physically and emotionally, but also spiritually, as we were doing this God's way and not the way of the world. I did find it hard and very stressful at first. In my naivety I thought I had been healed of depression; but a few months into our marriage I was to have a sudden depressive episode. It didn't help that Adrian was still very much on the scene with Lawson and in our lives. I had nothing against him and had a heart for him, but sometimes I struggled with his being around so much, especially as we were trying to establish our own family unit.

I was finding everything quite challenging; one afternoon I had gone up to the bedroom to get some alone time and to collect my thoughts, when an anger came over me and suddenly, as I would do in my past, I took it out on myself and hit the palm of my hands into my face. I didn't realise the force I must have hit myself with, as I gave myself a horrendous black eye. Julie was distraught when she saw it, and I broke down in sobs of tears as I tried to explain what happened. We went to the doctor and I was very emotional and really down. The doctor was really compassionate and supportive; I explained my past history and all the current events of being newly married, with the huge transition I had gone through. I agreed to go back onto medication to help balance me out, and to this day I still take them with no shame, knowing that the Lord uses medication to help people. I still pray to the Lord to heal me from depression, but He has never answered with a 'yes'. I also know sometimes His answer is no and he doesn't always heal people of everything they ask to be healed from. I do know that I trust Him and truly believe He allows the depression to remain, that I cling to Him and know my hope is in Him. But I also know that I can help myself against depression, by taking my medication, trying to eat right and training regularly. But the depression still sometimes comes without warning and there is never a warning when it does.

As time went on, I felt that the Lord was showing me and helping me in my times of needing affirmation and need to feel loved and wanted. I was to seek it first through Him and to turn to Him instead of trying to seek Julie to meet all my needs wants and expectations. It is still a journey and something I'm still learning, but Jesus was teaching us both to come to Him first and foremost. We were learning a new way of how to be intimate with each other without bringing old habits and behaviours or unhealthy thoughts and fantasies into the bedroom. We found that by coming before the Lord and seeking Him first in our time with each other, we were able to connect with each other beyond anything we could imagine. I was learning the art of communication, learning how to connect with Julie emotionally as well as physically. I admit that I am still learning and still struggle with opening up and talking and being completely vulnerable before Julie. One thing we agreed on early on and knew wasn't right before the Lord, was self-pleasure, especially when we were away from each other. People may say it's normal, that there's nothing wrong with it, but we both know that to have the blessing of the Lord upon our marriage and intimacy we needed to keep ourselves pure for each other, and self-pleasure robs of that, especially with the thoughts and fantasies that can go with it. As we were doing this God's way, we knew that when the urge would come, we should be intimate with each other and not go down the route of old habits by self-pleasuring. Without shame I can honestly admit that at times I have failed in this area; I am in need of Jesus like anyone else and at times I take my eyes off Him and that leads me to fail in areas of my life, especially in self-pleasure.

Honesty is paramount with me and Julie and I have sheepishly confessed when I have failed here. We pray together and I repent of it and in Jesus's strength I keep moving forward. In a Christian marriage it's important to learn to bring everything into the light and not keep secrets from each other. As a Christian Husband and father, I come under temptation just like any other male, but the key is in choosing to turn to Jesus when temptation comes and allow Him to give you the strength to resist. For example, as a man I am not immune when I see an attractive or beautiful woman, especially when I accidentally glance at one. What makes the difference is, if I happen to glance at a beautiful woman, it is choosing to deliberately look away. To not glance back at them and avoid eye contact and especially not to look where men would look. I also choose to remember that they are someone's precious daughter and I actually pray to Jesus in my head saying, "Lord, may they know their inner beauty and value in you as much as their outer beauty". I choose to only have eyes for Julie and for her body. It is also important to choose not to get involved with the vulgar talk that guys make about women when they are together, walking away when you hear it.

Julie and I strongly wanted her to become pregnant naturally, ideally with a daughter, but sadly it never happened. We seriously considered IVF, but with much prayer and consideration when we were at the referral with a doctor in Inverness, we believed that God was telling us not to go down this route. One blessing in not having another child was the time I was able to give solely to Lawson; it was precious, and we were able to truly bond in a father/son relationship. This certainly didn't come without its challenges, but I made sure that Lawson knew that he was loved. I wasn't going anywhere, although we went through times of him trying to push me away, testing to see if I truly loved him even when he was being horrible to me. But I loved him unconditionally and even though he wasn't my son biologically, he was my son all the same, given to me by Jesus Himself.

For the first few years of our marriage, it was hard, feeling isolated in spiritually speaking up in Newtonmore. We had no other Christian couple to help mentor and nurture us as we were first working this out. There was no church nearby; we were hungry for Jesus and we were willing to travel as far as Inverness or Perth each Sunday to be part of a fellowship, even though either way the journey on the A9 was an hour's drive. But during the week we had nothing to really be part of. Both of us were part of an evangelistic ministry and mentoring program, designed to help nurture and bring us on and mature us in our calling, but after we were first married, we believed God was asking us to step back from this program and ministry. We believed that we were to concentrate for the time being in establishing ourselves as a Christian couple and family and most importantly, in our individual relationships with Him. We were blessed to find another family who lived by in Aviemore that were also Christians. They were a South African couple with a couple of kids and were a great support to us in the early days of our marriage.

As time went on, we established ourselves as a family unit and would travel as far as Perth or

Inverness to the fellowship of a church. After a period of attending a church in Perth, we became part of the Destiny Church family in Inverness. Over the next few years it was important for Julie and me and our son Lawson to develop our relationship with Jesus on an individual level, as a married Christian couple and as a family. We were not involved with ministry or service for Jesus but just getting to know Him more intimately, for it was our heart towards Him that was more important than what we did for Him in service. We were being prepared for what He will one day call us to do for Him. We were blessed as a family where we lived, the childminding business my wife had and the kids we were fortunate to care for. I also had a job in a hotel I loved, and we lived in a lovely village. A door opened with an opportunity for me to work offshore as a steward, which brought financial blessing and an ability to give focussed quality time to my family when I was home, as I was working a three weeks on - three weeks off rota. I enjoyed my work offshore; it was great opportunity to share my faith with others and truly live out what I believed. A great many ex-servicemen work in the offshore industry with whom I could really connect, and the structure of offshore work and life was quite similar to that in the military.

After a few years' marriage, as a family we felt drawn to relocate and God opened the door for us to move nearer Perth; He brought the right buyer for our house and we also found the right house for us as a family in a beautiful village just outside Perth. We were now part a great fellowship and really felt the Lord's hand firmly upon us. When God opens a door, He can move very fast and we were uprooted and moved in a very short time. It was interesting as, at the time that we learned that the Lord wanted us to go to Perth, we had been trying to move to Edinburgh, feeling that it was to there we wanted to relocate.

But suddenly every door we pushed got firmly shut; trying to secure a mortgage, get a buyer for our own house and to buy the house we had our heart set on. We had setback after setback and we were getting very disheartened, especially when a potential buyer for our house in Newtonmore pulled out at the last minute. A friend said that maybe the Lord wanted us elsewhere and would we be open to that, when everything suddenly changed. Julie and I spent time seeking the Lord in prayer and said to God that if He wanted us to be in Perth, then please bring us a local buyer for whom this would be their 'forever' family home, and bring us a house just outside Perth in a beautiful village setting but in commuting distance of Perth. God answered our very requests. Online, we found and fell in love with the ideal home, that was suited for our very needs.

A family we knew from the village came and looked at our house and they even stated, "this could be our forever home." They put an offer in on the house. Our mortgage for the new house was secured. Doors opened and even our church in Perth loaned us a truck to move our belongings. We secured the purchase of the house we loved near Perth. God moved on our behalf and very quickly; nothing is too big or too small for Him and He is interested and involved in the most intricate of details in our lives if we let Him and trust Him. He delights in this. So, as a family under God's leading and guidance, we moved as a family from Newtonmore to Perthshire, to a new season and a new beginning. We had no idea what the future held for us, but it was exciting; God was in complete control and we trusted Him.

CONCLUSION

Since moving to Perthshire, these last few years have had their highs and lows, with the laughter, joy, tears, arguments and struggles that any other family goes through. But most importantly, through the darkest to the most glorious days, we have stuck together and got through as a family. I want to bring the book up to date with where I am and where we are as a family. As I'm writing this, the nation is going through the struggles of the Covid19 pandemic and it has been hard on all of us. Just because I'm a follower of Jesus doesn't mean I am exempt or immune to what is going on in this crazy world just now, so I will try to summarise my story in this concluding chapter and to thank you for persevering on the journey with me through this book.

It has not been easy, raising a stepson from youth to teenage years. It has been rewarding and enjoyable, but I admit it has also been very hard and like any dad, there are times I have wanted to pull my hair out and give my son a good shake; it has been an emotional journey together. There have been times when I have got it totally wrong; I have overreacted and been unfair. In my own stubbornness I have dug my heels in and said "no" when there was no need to. At times I felt a failure, failing my wife and my son with my own insecurities. There have been times of real ugliness where I have said or done things that I'm ashamed of. But through all the difficulty episodes with my son, I have always reassured him that I love him; that he is my son no matter what, and that I am never going anywhere.

My son has had his own struggles over the years and there have been situations when he has tried to push me away, to see if I will still love him at his worst and most unlovable. I may be a little biased here, in saying that when a child is your birth child it is easier to love them than if they are a stepchild. I believe that it is harder to love a child that is not yours biologically, but also that in ways it can be more rewarding to be a dad to that child (these are my own thoughts, not a statement of fact.)

I have always told my son that is he is <u>my</u> son all the same and I love him as if he is my very own birth child. The good outweighs the bad every time; I have seen my son grow into an outstanding, confident, polite, gentle, compassionate helpful, thoughtful and amazing young man. He towers over me, made of pure muscle, fit and strong and plans to embark on a career in the military in time to come. I have always tried to support my son and encourage him in all that he does. The military is of his own choosing and I have always told him I am behind him and I have his back. I asked my son if I could adopt him and he said he would like me to. My wife Julie is totally behind me and as I write this, we are going through the process of adoption. I don't need a piece of paper to tell me he is my son, but I feel that this is icing on the cake of our relationship. I can now officially say he's mine and that's it – and now he cannot escape! Joking aside, he is my son and I love him, and I am so blessed to be his dad.

Julie and I were unable to conceive naturally, my low sperm count and sperm mobility issues which affecting the ability to conceive. A few years ago, as a family, including my son, we decided we would try the route of adoption. Fostering was not an option, as we both knew we couldn't cope with having to let a child go back into the system or to a new family; this would be too heart-breaking. I used to say with a laugh, that it was hard to even hand back the children we childminded let alone a foster child. Adoption was our only option. We went through the process with Barnardos and it wasn't easy. It would clearly be a long thorough process and a very emotional journey for both of us. I can understand why; the last thing any adoption organisation is going to do is to simply hand a child over to any family. We were assigned a great social worker who would take us through the process. It was hard and every area of our lives was exposed and discussed, to make sure we were suitable to be adoptive parents.

We learned that the majority of children in the care system who are looking to be adopted may have issues and struggle with emotion and behaviour. There may be a history of abuse from birth families and parents. It was heart-breaking to hear and to learn all about it as we went through the process. They had to be honest and real with us that the adoption would be the easy part; it would be the bonding and living as a new family that would bring the heartache and the struggles. I suppose they had to give us the gritty story first to establish if we were up to the task. Julie and I were still keen and determined to give a child a new home, a new start and a family that would love them. The background checks were intense, especially with my own mental health history. I had to retrieve my medical records from my military days. There was no discrimination against my own past; my case worker just needed to prove I was robust nowadays and to prove that I would be able to be an adoptive father. The size and extent of my medical records quite took me back and it was an emotional and tearful journey to read through them all.

I got to see what the doctors had written about me, back in my darkest days as a soldier. I got angry and I cried - it was painful to see what had been written. It took me back and brought back memories I didn't even remember having, of accounts of things I had done. Maybe I chose to forget about them; instances of trying to throw myself in front of a car, or to drown myself in the sea at Lossiemouth. Reading these brought it all back like it was yesterday. I sat and I cried and felt broken again. But I wasn't truly broken; I realised that this was an opportunity to bring closure where I thought there was none, to let go more, to forgive where I needed to forgive. It was also an opportunity of healing and release. If these reports were read for the first time without knowing who I was or the journey I have been on, no one in their right mind would let me adopt a child let alone be allowed to walk the streets unsupervised. Barnardos were great - my medical files didn't stop the process. Our case worker advised us that it would support our application if we sought counselling, allowing the official records to show the selection board that we were doing all things possible and to demonstrate our commitment. We went to a three-day adoption preparation course in Glasgow to equip and prepare us for adoption. This was an eye-opener but also really helpful, as it really got down to the detail of everything to do with adoption and the realities of it.

After the course we attended counselling and had regular visits from our case worker. At this point of the emotional journey, I started to have doubts and shared my heart with Julie. She was of similar mind and that was when we decided to step back from the process and eventually decided to give up our plans for adoption. I don't regret applying and I don't regret not adopting; this was a journey I felt we needed to try but it just wasn't meant to be. I don't have any regrets at not being able to have a child of my own; I am content that I have my stepson and my wife, and I am thankful for all that I have.

Soon after moving to Perthshire another blessing came into our lives. 'Humbug' had been the family dog, but he was a man's dog and had really been my dog from the start. My son and Julie talked me into going to look at a female puppy that was available. 'Ruby' as we called her, was another King Charles Cavalier like Humbug, but she was ruby in colour hence the name. I didn't want to get her at first, but she was meant to be a companion to Humbug and also to be Julie's dog. She was very beautiful, and we couldn't resist getting her. Unfortunately, she was also to be a man's dog and I ended up with two loyal dogs. To this day Julie jokingly says that I stole Ruby's affection be whispering sweet nothings into her ear at night. She has become my wee princess and a very jealous dog, with a great character and loyal affection. In the mornings when I sit down in my chair to have my morning coffee, I have a pair of canine bookends sitting on me, getting their cuddle time. We sit there and put the world to right as I drink my coffee. These two dogs are a real blessing from God, and they give the most amazing unconditional love. The Lord knew I always wanted a dog of my very own and He blessed me with two.

As I bring this book to a close, I have been reflecting on what an incredible journey I have been on. I can truly say that I can now see where God has been instrumental in my life, where He has intervened and where His hand has been directly upon me. He showed up in my life and revealed Himself to me when I wasn't even looking for Him. I know there will be many who read this book, who will have no desire for God or even believe He is real. Regardless of this, my hope is that this will be a book that will inspire, encourage and help someone. A light that will shine into the darkness of someone's despair and show there is hope.

As a follower of Jesus, I am in no way perfect or even 'have it all together'. I am someone who struggles like everyone else. Someone who battles depression, mental health, insecurities, anger, and so on. What makes me different to others? It is simply this; I have come to know and truly experience the love, grace, mercy, forgiveness and acceptance of Jesus Christ. He offers to all what He offered me. All He requires is you simply believe; believe in Him and what He did at the Cross of Calvary.

I write in my journal each day just three words. Three words that remind me of who I am and how I receive His love.

BELIEVE. RECEIVE. BECOME.

I want to end with just one scripture that for me is a life verse:

John 1:12(ESV)

"But to all who did receive Him, who believed in His name, He gave the right to become children of God."

Thank you for taking time to read this book, if this book has impacted you in anyway and you would like to contact me:

mcewenbruce@yahoo.co.uk

Photos:

Printed in Great Britain
by Amazon